Rock Creek Park

One must be acutely sorry for him who has not been lost in this dearest of city wildernesses.

—Robert L. Dickinson, 1918

Rock Creek Park

Gail Spilsbury

The Johns Hopkins University Press

Baltimore and London

This book has been brought to publication through the generous assistance of J. Kent Minichiello and Anthony W. White.

Copyright © 2003 The Johns Hopkins University Press

All rights reserved. Published 2003
Printed in China on acid-free paper
9 8 7 6 5 4 3 2 1

The Johns Hopkins University Press
2715 North Charles Street
Baltimore, MD 21218-4363
www.press.jhu.edu

Library of Congress Control Number: 2003100403
A catalog record for this book is available from the British Library.

Designed by Yael Kats, Gazelle

Cover: *Rock Creek* © 2002 Maxwell MacKenzie. All rights reserved. Reproduction prohibited without written permission: 2641 Garfield Street, NW, Washington, DC 20008.

Back cover: *Kalmia,* by Ivana Kučan, 2002. Gouache on paper. Courtesy of the author. Olmsted Brothers signature, photograph © 2002 Herman Woerner. Courtesy of the National Park Service, Frederick Law Olmsted National Historic Site.

Half-title page: Quotation from Robert L. Dickinson, "Washington Walk Book," 1918, unpublished manuscript, Robert L. Dickinson Papers, Manuscript Division, Library of Congress. Photograph by E. C. Whiting for the Rock Creek Park Report of 1918, June 6, 1917, with caption: "A bit of Rock Creek beauty which must not be injured. But there should be better opportunities to appreciate such scenes by skillfully managed openings in the foliage screen and by well devised location of foot-paths, bridle paths, and roads." Courtesy of the National Park Service, Frederick Law Olmsted National Historic Site. 2837-9

Title page: *Snow Scene Rock Creek Park,* undated photograph, by Maj. Ulysses S. Grant III (1881–1969). Courtesy of the Historical Society of Washington, D.C.

Dedication page: *Treetops with Clouds in Rock Creek Park,* ca. 1920–1950, by Theodor Horydczak (ca. 1890–1971). Courtesy of the Library of Congress, Prints and Photographs Collection.

Page vi: *Rock Creek through the Trees,* ca. 1920–1950, by Theodor Horydczak (ca. 1890–1971). Courtesy of the Library of Congress, Prints and Photographs Collection.

Quotation on page 31: Frederick Law Olmsted Jr. and John Nolen, "The Normal Requirements of American Towns and Cities in Respect to Public Open Spaces," *Charities and the Commons,* 16, no. 14 (July 1906): 424.

Endpapers: Photograph from the Rock Creek Park Report of 1918. Courtesy of the National Park Service, Frederick Law Olmsted National Historic Site. 2837-52

To Bobby and Joseph

Contents

Rock Creek Park is universally treasured by Washingtonians. Its 1,754 acres have always been a place to roam or recreate, surrounded by quiet, natural beauty. Tall trees and steep slopes characterize the park, and paths wind through its sylvan landscapes much in the manner of its meandering stream. Over more than a century, many Washingtonians, including presidents, have voiced their love for and personal ownership of this wooded retreat and have supported its conservation. This precedent for preserving the park's integrity—its nativity—under the crush of an important metropolis ever consuming as it grows is something precious about Rock Creek Park and must remain its mandate for the future as natural and man-made threats intensify.

This book began when I visited Frederick Law Olmsted's historic home in Brookline, Massachusetts. The home and studio space of the father of landscape architecture in the United States is now a museum, archive, and education center under the jurisdiction of the National Park Service. As I toured the Olmsted firm's workshop and marveled at the early-twentieth-century implements and strange-looking printing machine, I noticed a book on display entitled Rock Creek Park. It turned out to be the Rock Creek Park Report of 1918 prepared by Olmsted's son, Frederick Law Olmsted Jr., for Rock Creek Park's managers. I began to read the report and was immediately struck by the passionate and refreshingly quaint descriptions of the park's natural beauty that "must be saved intact insofar as possible." It was exciting to discover that our own, much loved Rock Creek Park had an important Olmsted connection. Portions of the report seemed relevant to both the park and Washingtonians today, although nearly a century had passed. Although the report served at one time as a guide for the park's development and maintenance—where to weed, clear, plant, build roads, or extend borders—it also stands, forever, as a platform for the park's preservation as a natural landscape. Indeed it has been invoked over the years to prevent park intrusions, including proposals in the 1960s and '70s for a four-lane highway to cut through the valley. The report is still in use today as the National Park Service conducts studies on the park's historic integrity, for it presents an excellent inventory of the early century's vegetation.

I began this project wanting to share the Rock Creek Park Report (also called the Olmsted Report) with Washington-

Bows, 1999, by Elżbieta Sikorska, graphite on paper, 45 x 34 in. Courtesy of the artist.

ians, who I imagined would be as interested as I in the park's Olmsted connection. As soon as I started research into the Rock Creek Park Report, it was apparent that a web of stories related to it: the founding of the park itself in 1890; the melded histories of the park, city beautification, and urban planning movements of the nineteenth and early twentieth centuries; the Olmsted continuum in these movements; and finally, the riveting advent, in 1902, of the so-called McMillan Plan for Washington's improvement, for which Frederick Law Olmsted Jr. prepared the park portion. His visionary park system mapped out in the McMillan Plan was the precursor for the Rock Creek Park Report of 1918. And so, these many strands of history needed to accompany a presentation of Olmsted Jr.'s Rock Creek Park Report. My aim has been to condense these stories into a visual commemoration of the park—our park—because we who see it daily and use it frequently, or only occasionally, love it and hope its beauty will always be safeguarded. Besides the remarkable continuum connected to the park's history, the public's appreciation of it is another continuum, and the one that is the most important for the park's lasting integrity.

Although most people today do not know who Frederick Law Olmsted Sr. was, those who do, admire him not only for his rich legacy in landscape architec-

ture projects and for his role in creating a collective attitude toward our nation's landscapes but also for his leadership in public life. His work and pursuits involved many of the issues of his day, from slavery to city planning to the establishment of national parks. His firm, carried on by his sons Frederick Jr. and John, ultimately contributed to more than five thousand landscape projects in the United States. Anyone paging through the firm's Master List of Design Projects will undoubtedly recognize a university, public park, private residence, suburban development, or municipal building landscaped by the Olmsteds. New York's Central and Prospect parks and Boston's Emerald Necklace park system are the most famous works. Public service became as much a family tradition as the landscape business for the Olmsteds. Frederick Jr. is known for devoting immeasurable personal time to the plan for Washington and its implementation. This book, in addition to paying homage to Rock Creek Park with the hope of encouraging its continued conservation by the public and government, also commemorates the Olmsteds, whose unsurpassed service toward developing our public landscapes and national values about them—our landscape culture—deserves perpetual recognition.

Many scholars have studied the Olmsteds, the McMillan Plan, the capital city, and Rock Creek Park, and their works are listed in the bibliography on page 73. What follows touches only upon the highlights of each of these deeper histories, but attempts to provide the reader with a pleasurable glimpse of the rich, historical vein and remarkable legacy created by these intertwining stories and their leaders.

OLMSTED BROTHERS

LANDSCAPE ARCHITECTS

Comprehensive Land Planning

Letterhead Olmsted firm, photograph © 2002 Herman Woerner. Courtesy of the National Park Service, Frederick Law Olmsted National Historic Site.

1 | The Park: Past, Present, Future

A Brief Look at the Past

Until George Washington formally identified the location for the nation's capital city in 1790, the steep, wooded, and rocky valley that became Rock Creek Park one hundred years later was uninhabited land, although Native American tribes used the area for game and other resources. European settlers, particularly Scotch-Irish, came to the capital area in the late 1600s and developed tobacco farming, although not in the park's craggy ravines. One Henry Darnell held a land grant of 6,000 acres, which included all of today's Rock Creek Park.

Within several generations, the area surrounding Rock Creek Park had become a trading post for tobacco and wheat farmers, with Georgetown and Alexandria serving as ports. The name Potomac derives from the Algonquian word for "something brought," or loosely, "trading place." At the lower end of Rock Creek, near Georgetown, flour and grist mills developed as part of the burgeoning economy. The creek was navigable as far as P Street, but the park proper, as we know it today, remained mostly forested with a handful of landowners, of which several families owned large tracts. The Peirces

owned the most land and are probably the only family remembered today by local residents, perhaps solely because Peirce Mill still stands and is now a tourist attraction. Joshua Peirce (1795–1869), son of the family patriarch, Isaac Peirce (1756–1841), built the stone mansion off Porter Street that now houses National Park Service offices and is known as the Klingle Mansion. Joshua Peirce was a prominent and wealthy horticulturist with greenhouses and a nursery on his landscaped property, which he named Linnaean Hill after the Swedish botanist Carl von Linne. Peirce was particularly known for his camellias, a rarity at the time, and his nurseries may have provided plants for the presidential mansion, Capitol Hill, and other federal and public grounds.

Thomas Blagden (1815–1870), another large landowner and prominent miller in Rock Creek Valley, is remembered today by the street named after him—Blagden Avenue—located a short distance north of Peirce Mill. The ruins of the Blagden Mill, also called the Argyle Mill after the name on the original land patent, were removed in 1899 during the construction of Beach Drive. When Congress established Rock Creek Park

Early 20th-century photograph of Klingle Ford. Courtesy of the Historical Society of Washington, D.C.

in 1890, about seventy people held title to land in the park, with several families still holding the largest tracts.

The capital city's mills built along the Chesapeake and Ohio Canal flourished during the first half of the nineteenth century, while Rock Creek Park's eight mills were less profitable because they lacked ready access to central docks and transit lines. The Columbian Mill, once standing on National Zoo land, may have been built in the late 1700s by the Georgetown entrepreneur Benjamin Stoddert, for whom the District's community soccer program is named. In 1825, John Quincy Adams purchased the mill, and it became known as Adams Mill, the namesake for today's well-traveled Adams Mill Road.

Washington's mills declined over the second half of the nineteenth century for various reasons, including Baltimore's rise as the area's largest port. In addition, as the new capital city sprouted up, real estate superseded mills as the most profitable industry. Finally, in the Midwest, a new process for milling wheat rendered water-powered mills obsolete and moved the milling center to a different part of the country.

The Civil War marked a turning point in the District's history and also affected Rock Creek Park's northern landscape, where in 1862 large forest tracts were cut down to build Military Road and Fort DeRussy, and create sight lines for the fort's guns. In 1863, forty-eight forts ringed the city, joined in the northern part and through Rock Creek Park by a 1.5-mile swath of stump-strewn land. During the war, Fort DeRussy, the highest point in the park, staved off a Confederate advance through Rock Creek Valley in the so-called Battle of Fort Stevens of mid-July 1864. As a result of the war, Military Road became a major east-west traffic corridor through the park. Its bridge, just below the creek's older Milk House Ford, offered a safer and more reliable transit route.

Washington's population doubled during the Civil War period, setting off unprecedented suburban growth and crowding the city proper. The white population grew from 40,000 in 1850 to 109,000 in 1870, while the black population increased from 10,000 to 35,000. Farms adjacent to Rock Creek Valley were platted and subdivided into new neighborhoods, including Mount Pleasant Village (1865) and Meridian Hill (1867).

Somewhat later, streetcar lines to the northwest spurred development of other communities on both sides of today's park—Petworth (1887), Chevy Chase (1890), Brightwood (1891), and Cleveland Park (1894).

Long before 1866, the year that official efforts to create a major park for Washington began, residents had already discovered the mesmerizing beauty and recreational potential of Rock Creek Valley. People made use of the transit routes and bridle paths that crisscrossed the picturesque ravines, and pleasure drives in carriages afforded a welcome escape not only from daily life but also

Opposite: Rock Creek Sunday, 2000, by Mary F. Kokoski, acrylic on paper. Courtesy of the artist.

Above: Footbridge, from the Rock Creek Park Report of 1918. Courtesy of the National Park Service, Frederick Law Olmsted National Historic Site. 2837-49

from Washington's increasingly unhealthy conditions brought on by rapid city growth and crowding. The Washington Canal, which once paralleled today's Constitution Avenue, had become an open sewer by the 1860s, and as late as 1881 only one-third of Washington's houses were connected to sewers, so that a majority of residents depended on wells and springs that often became contaminated.[1] The urban park movement of the era, which advocated open spaces in cities for exercise, health, and an aesthetic change from city squalor, led residents, including President and Mrs. Lincoln, to seek relief in the surrounding countryside.

Yet, passing legislation to create Rock Creek Park was not easy and took twenty-five years of intermittent lobbying on the part of dedicated congressmen and civic leaders to achieve success. Although the urban park movement—headed in large part by Frederick Law Olmsted (1822–1903)—influenced public support for a natural preserve in the capital city, it was the pestilential condition of President Lincoln's own residence that catalyzed action. To escape Washington's unhealthy conditions, the Lincolns frequently retreated to Soldiers Home, a large park that today faces the Washington Hospital Center. The chief executive's preference for this green space with fresh air led to an official survey and report on suitable land for a new presidential mansion and surrounding park. In 1866, Maj. Nathaniel Michler of the U.S. Army Corps of Engineers undertook the survey. His report, submitted the following year, offered less material on the proposed presidential mansion than on Rock Creek's unparalleled attributes for becoming a grand city park. His writing was inspired by the same features that delight park visitors today:

All the elements which constitute a public resort of the kind can be found in this wild and romantic tract of country. With its charming drives and walks, its hills and dales, its pleasant valleys and deep ravines, its primeval forests and cultivated fields, its running waters, its rocks clothed with rich fern and

mosses, its repose and tranquility, its light and shade, its ever-varying shrubbery, its beautiful and extensive views, the locality is already possessed with all the features necessary for the object in view. [2]

Although no legislation for Rock Creek Park resulted from Michler's work, his report has endured to the present day, as park planners and historians review the continuum of individuals involved in creating and preserving one of the country's most remarkable natural landscapes within an intense urban environment.

The next significant initiatives toward park legislation began in the early 1880s, spearheaded by civic leadership. Several Senate bills were defeated in the House, underscoring a problem that capital city improvements had faced from the day the District became the seat of government: congressmen who did not want their distant constituencies made responsible for building and maintaining the city. [3]

Charles Carroll Glover (1846–1936), remembered today for Glover Park north of Georgetown, accomplished much for Washington in the realm of land preservation. Not only did he donate his personal property for several city parks, he also devoted himself to the creation—from ugly mudflats—of East and West Potomac parks, those graceful, green spaces curving along Washington's waterfront and later ennobled by the Lincoln and Jefferson

Opposite: Columbian Mill, Rock Creek Park, 1874, by James Madison Alden (1834–1922). Watercolor on paper. Courtesy of Sarah Alden Hern Turner. Descended from the Pilgrims, Washington-area landscape artist James Madison Alden painted watercolors for the United States Coastal Survey and documented such historic times as the Gold Rush in California, the Oregon Territory in 1857, Puget Sound, and Canada in the days of the Hudson Bay Company. He also painted Rock Creek Park when at home.

Above: From the Rock Creek Park Report of 1918, with caption: "Upstream from footbridge above Boulder Bridge," 1917. Courtesy of the National Park Service, Frederick Law Olmsted National Historic Site. 2837-1

memorials. Glover and other civic leaders also dedicated themselves to passage of the Zoological Bill in 1889, which created the National Zoo. Yet for all these remarkable achievements for the city's beautification, Glover's crowning glory was his role as leading lobbyist for Rock Creek Park. [4] Although some Washingtonians today know who Charles Glover was—particularly those who escape to Glover Park—the majority are unaware that he was president of Riggs Bank, the Washington Stock Exchange, and the Corcoran Gallery of Art over the course of a long life intimately tied to civic improvements.

In the city's historical records, the story is often told of how Glover rallied support for Rock Creek Park legislation by taking political contacts out for a horseback ride in the park on Thanksgiving Day 1888. The tour of the park's sylvan beauty ended with a pledge by all present to strive unceasingly for park legislation. Crosby Noyes, editor of the *Evening Star* and a member of the committee Glover subsequently formed to lobby Congress, wrote editorials to increase public pressure for the park initiative.

Notable among the series of failed legislative efforts to create Rock Creek Park was a March 1890 bill that called for naming the park Columbus Memorial Park in commemoration of the approaching quadricentennial of Columbus's discovery of America. [5]

Finally, both houses passed the Rock Creek Park Bill on September 25, 1890. The act's opening paragraph authorized that specified land "shall be secured, as hereinafter set out, and be perpetually dedicated and set apart as a public park or pleasure ground for the benefit and enjoyment of the people of the United States, to be known by the name Rock Creek Park." [6] Over the next two years, the park's first administrative body overcame untold financial and legal hurdles in order to acquire the designated land for park use. It had been a tumultuous beginning for the park, one involving many political battles, but the peaceful territory stretching from the zoo's northern border to the District line, and lying roughly between Sixteenth Street on the East and Broad Branch Road and Oregon Avenue on the West, came under federal protection for all time. That was not to say it would simply exist without future threats to its sovereignty; much lay ahead, and still does, making the landscape we enjoy today all the more spectacular for its remarkable survival.

Incarnating "City Beautiful"

In 1900, Frederick Law Olmsted Jr. (1870–1957) formally began his long association with the development and beautification of Washington, D.C., which included an intimate and sustained relationship with Rock Creek Park, consecrated by his Rock Creek Park Report of

1918, also called the Olmsted Report. The Olmsteds—father and sons—provided a continuum of park and city development in Washington, D.C., that paralleled larger national movements of the day. Frederick Law Olmsted Sr. was a principal leader of the mid-nineteenth-century urban park movement and designed New York's Central Park (1858) and Prospect Park (1866). His firm also conceived the regional park system, best exemplified by Boston's Emerald Necklace, begun in the mid-1870s. Olmsted Sr. consulted regularly on Washington's planning, contributed to the design of the Capitol grounds, and even wrote a preamble to an early bill to establish Rock Creek Park. Olmsted Jr. carried on his family's involvement and led Washington into the next generation—and century—of urban park and city planning developments. He distinguished himself by becoming a central figure in the turn-of-the-century city beautiful movement, an outgrowth of the earlier city park movement. Olmsted Jr. exerted even more influence than this, for his early initiatives toward Washington's beautification naturally led him to prominent involvement in the nascent urban planning field. He also contributed significantly to the broader national park movement and the establishment of the National Park Service. The nation's embracement of the notion of national parks to preserve natural landscapes also intersected with the establishment of Rock Creek Park, for several important tracts of land became national parks around the same time, including Yosemite, which the elder Olmsted had reported on years before. Rock Creek Park's formation thus embodies the major landscape movements of the nineteenth century: urban parks, city beautification, and national parks—movements spearheaded, always with modesty, by the Olmsteds.

Maintaining the Park

Today, under the guardianship of the National Park Service, Rock Creek Park's Olmsted tradition continues. An attitude of preserving and restoring, where possible, the park's natural attributes guides decision making. Prevention of any further major land clearing for new structures or roads is a Park Service objective. The research staff continually studies and documents the park's ever-evolving vegetation, and the information garnered from this close observation has revealed the park's remarkable historic integrity, a promising condition for future generations to uphold. The Olmsted firm's reconnaissance work for the Report of 1918 has provided a rich portrait of the park's vegetation in the early part of the twentieth century. Thus subsequent changes over the century can be observed and evaluated. The cultural landscape inventory documents for future management purposes the park's defining

Trees Casting Long Shadows in Rock Creek Park, ca. 1920–1950, by Theodor Horydczak (ca. 1890–1971). Courtesy of the Library of Congress, Prints and Photographs Collection.

characteristics in terms of historic integrity. These features include views, circulation system (trails, bridle paths, roads, parking lots), clustered buildings (Peirce Mill), and large clearings, such as the golf course, tennis court complex, and Carter Barron Amphitheatre. In terms of landscape principles, the Park Service plan adheres to the Olmsted model, which is to study what exists—as landscape vegetation naturally evolves—and manage accordingly. [7]

Future Threats

To cope with the encroachments of ever-growing urbanization and the vicissitudes of natural phenomena, the Park Service has created a general management plan to guide decision making over the early decades of the twenty-first century. Previously, personal opinion, politics, and special interest groups influenced park management. With an official, published guide, the Park Service is able to efficiently handle the continuous flow of both good and bad ideas for the park's use.

What are today's principal threats to the park's preservation? Border encroachments have always been a problem, whittling away the park's total acreage. At present, more than one hundred encroachment violations need to be settled. Another danger is cell phone towers. Already two towers have been built, one at the maintenance facility and another at the tennis center, both high points in the park. The

Park Service's policy is to review cell phone tower applications on a case-by-case basis and from the standpoint that allowing their presence sets a dangerous precedent for similar encroachments. Invasive exotics also must be checked if the park's indigenous plants are to remain. The creek, too, must receive better protection from abuses that include littering, storm runoff contamination, and chemical spills. The park's existing historic structures, such as Peirce Mill, have fallen into disrepair as a result of insufficient funds for their upkeep. A citizens group, Friends of Peirce Mill, has been raising funds to restore the mill. Finally, the most pressing issue facing Rock Creek Park today can be summed up in a single word: traffic. Commuters want more roads, and recreational users want existing roads permanently closed. Hikers, bikers, and dog walkers lobby for special trails suitable for their activities, and pressure continually mounts for more ball fields. Competition for the available space often overshadows the sheer miracle that Washington residents have the gift of that sylvan space at all. Therefore, the Park Service's general management plan creates a record of what will and will not be pursued in the park in order to preserve historic integrity. [8]

Two hundred years ago Rock Creek Park was the uninhabited place it remains today, only its borders once fed into endless countryside and its appearance was more pristine. Its topography saved it from the early suburbanization that transformed the rest of Washington after the Civil War, but only an Act of Congress spared it from the subsequent waves of housing development; its wooded slopes and spectacular views would have become prime real estate for the wealthy.

The park has always been a part of Washington, even before its official decree, and it belongs to the city's collective memory. It is all too easy to assume that it rests there, awaiting our visits, offering its tall trees, deep sky, inspiring hillsides, and untamed meadows with views. It would be wiser to face the truth that public leadership and a large endowment are urgently needed to allow the Park Service, and citizens groups, to nurture an urban park whose current ailments are likely to become irreversible with ever-consuming urban growth over the next hundred years. How much we value this park is a story that will continue to evolve.

A Stream in Rock Creek Park, ca. 1909–1932, from the National Photo Company. Courtesy of the Library of Congress, Prints and Photographs Collection.

2 | The McMillan Plan of 1902

The advent of the so-called McMillan Plan of 1902 for the replanning of Washington, D.C., is rich in historic significance; it also had a direct impact on Rock Creek Park and illuminates a fascinating continuum in the history of American city parks, urban planning, and the Olmsteds, down to the present-day centenary of the plan's acceptance by the House and Senate District committees. The "Report of the Senate Park Committee on the District of Columbia on the Improvement of the Park System of the District of Columbia"—nicknamed the McMillan Plan for Senator James McMillan of Michigan who chaired the Senate District Committee—was a report, not legislation, but it served for decades as the blueprint for Washington's development, and it continues to exert influence today. Just as the McMillan Plan was an extension of Maj. Pierre Charles L'Enfant's original design of 1791, so the plans for Washington's monumental core and park system over the past one hundred years have continued to reflect the vision of these earlier documents. Frederick Law Olmsted Jr. served on the Commission of Fine Arts from its creation in 1910 until 1918; this agency implemented many features of the McMillan Plan and continues to approve new buildings and monuments for the city. Olmsted Jr. also served as the first president of the National Capital Park and Planning Commission (1926), successor agency to the National Capital Park Commission (1924). Both agencies were responsible for developing the regional park system based on the guidelines presented in both the McMillan Plan and the 1918 Olmsted Report. While the McMillan Plan made broad suggestions for Rock Creek Park and a larger, interconnected park system—influenced by the Olmsted firm's design for Boston's Emerald Necklace of linked city parks—the Olmsted Report went further and offered a detailed study with specific recommendations for the park's improvement and preservation as a natural setting for public use. The McMillan Plan, followed by the Rock Creek Park Report—with Olmsted Jr. a principal force behind both—is but one of the fascinating continuums distinguishing Washington, D.C.'s development.

The need for public parks and the concept of beautifying cities gained unstoppable momentum in mid-nineteenth-century America. Frederick Law Olmsted Sr. led the park movement through his writings and projects, Central

Winter scene, undated photograph, from the *Star* Collection, copyright *Washington Post,* permission of the D.C. Public Library.

geoning America's desire for well-ordered, beautiful cities. Where could lower-income residents get fresh air, exercise, and the restorative attributes of rural scenery when their economic condition confined them to unhealthy city neighborhoods devoid of open spaces? As a new and ambitious nation, what could be done to make our fast-growing metropolises compare to the beauty and majesty of great European cities? The seeds for urban planning were inherent in the mid-century park movement led by the elder Frederick Law Olmsted. At the end of his life, with his crowning project, the resplendent neoclassical World's Columbian Exposition in Chicago in 1893, which set off the country's city beautiful movement, Olmsted passed the torch to his son Frederick Jr. In 1900, Olmsted Jr. helped to organize Harvard University's school of landscape architecture, where he also taught and later offered the first course in city planning. In this remarkable continuum of park, city beautification, and urban planning movements, Washington, D.C., became the foremost beneficiary, with the blueprint for its development contained in the McMillan Plan, for which Olmsted Jr. did much of the drafting.

Park (1858) being the first and most famous, and successfully crusaded for recognition of the profession of landscape architecture. The industrial revolution, with its impact on the growth of cities with crowded, working-class populations, fed the public park movement, as did bur-

Giving birth to the McMillan Plan was no straightforward accomplishment, but rather stands as a riveting example of politics. Personalities, leadership, and clever strategizing—even deal-making—led to a design for Washington that resulted in one of the most beautiful city centers in the world. In 1900, Washington was young—one hundred years old—and over the first decades of its growth, the work of government to steer a fledgling country had placed city improvements in a position of low priority, with the result that city planners unevenly adhered to the inspired L'Enfant plan. The Civil War marked a turning point in Washington's history because of its dramatic effect on the city's population growth and subsequent urban development, so that from mid-century on, the L'Enfant plan receded from view.

L'Enfant's design included a grand, formal avenue stretching from the Capitol to the site of the Washington Monument, but by the time of the Civil War, this long strip, today's Mall, had become a series of individual gardens with trees and winding paths. Another major problem was the Pennsylvania Railroad's station on the Mall and tracks crossing the Mall at Sixth Street. The Federal Triangle area—at that time the city's squalid Center Market—was nicknamed Murder Bay.

Two principal events set the wheels in motion for the McMillan Plan: the World's Columbian Exposition and the approaching centennial celebration of Washington, D.C., in 1900. The Chicago Fair, as the exposition was commonly known, sparked national interest in city planning and created the criteria for it.

City plans would be based on strong axial relationships on a grand scale, with classical architecture that reflected the noble character of ancient cities such as Rome. The city beautiful movement that evolved embodied a leadership that provided continuity over many decades. Two prominent architects, Daniel H. Burnham and Charles F. McKim, were designers of the Chicago Fair, with Augustus Saint-Gaudens serving as sculptor and Olmsted Sr. as landscape architect. These same individuals, with Olmsted Jr. replacing his aged father, formed the U.S. Senate Park Commission, or McMillan Commission, a few years later. Thus, a special continuity in city design theory solidified over the course of the 1890s. The Chicago and Washington models strongly influenced the growth and development of many American cities and placed Olmsted Jr. at the forefront of the city planning movement.

The approach of Washington's centennial in the wake of the Chicago Fair's impact on city beautification led to a flurry of meetings among city dignitaries and the federal government to decide what major commemorative structure to build, be it a permanent memorial or a bridge across the Potomac to Arlington Cemetery. Senator James McMillan was involved in the centennial celebration negotiations from their beginning in 1898.

Simultaneously, another important figure in Washington's development was con-

From the Rock Creek Park Report of 1918, with caption: "A path in the northerly part of the Park that is unusually happy in its location and treatment; it even adds to the beauty of the spot. It has a quality of line and a harmony with its surroundings which could be much more generally secured if greater skill and care were used in such details." Courtesy of the National Park Service, Frederick Law Olmsted National Historic Site. 2837-32

tributing to sound solutions for the city's future design. Architect Glenn Brown, secretary of the American Institute of Architects (AIA) and author of a history of the U.S. Capitol, devoted himself to preventing passage of inferior plans for Washington, including one by his ultimate ally Senator McMillan, who as a politician had other interests to serve, most importantly, the railroads. McMillan's plan would have allowed a railroad station on the Mall. While battles raged over two plans for the Mall, presented by McMillan and Col. Theodore A. Bingham, chief of the Office of Public Buildings and Grounds of the Army Engineers, Glenn Brown strategized an opposing approach that ended up succeeding. He saw the city's centennial as a golden opportunity not only to hold the AIA's annual meeting in Washington, with its theme of the city's future plan, but also to call upon the members' expertise to come up with fresh visions for the monumental core, based on the L'Enfant plan. Brown had no doubts that the nation's best architects would propose ideas far superior to the ones about to be considered by Congress. Among those who presented designs were Cass Gilbert, Paul J. Pelz, George O. Totten Jr., and Edgar Seeler. Olmsted Jr. presented a now famous paper on the role of landscape architecture in the improvement of cities, which expressed ideas carried over from his father's landscape tradition, tenets

that would guide both the McMillan and Rock Creek Park reports later on:

Wherever in a public park the primary motif of providing this quiet rural scenery seems to have been deliberately, wisely, and thoughtfully chosen, I should steadfastly oppose the introduction into it of any unnecessary building, though it were championed by every architect of the Institute; because the enjoyment it might afford would be of that civic sort from which it was the purpose of that park to afford a change. [9]

The ideas presented at the AIA meeting of 1900 contributed to the future McMillan Commission's work as its members developed a comprehensive plan for Washington. During the AIA's meeting, a committee formed and collaborated with Senator McMillan to gain congressional approval for the president to appoint a professional commission to study the Mall and the city's park system and make suggestions for their improvement. This resolution failed in the House, principally because of Illinois Senator Joseph Cannon's unrelenting opposition to spending taxpayers' money on public art or architecture. At this point, Senator McMillan proved a wilier politician. He won approval for a new Senate resolution calling for a study of the District's park system that would be paid for by the Senate. That way, no House approval for

the measure was necessary. McMillan always intended the study to include a plan for the Mall's development but cloaked this objective in a "park study" and protected the plan's implementation by restricting it to a Senate-funded project. Thus, the McMillan Commission was born, which, in retrospect, was also the rebirthing of Washington, D.C.

As the next year began, an amazing story full of inspiration, momentum, personalities, creative genius, and Washington politics unfolded and culminated triumphantly on January 15, 1902, with the unveiling, in the Corcoran Gallery of Art, of a remarkable plan for the city's monumental core and regional park system. In a short period of time—from April 1901 to January 1902—the McMillan Commission accomplished a prodigious amount of work, attesting to the inspiration that propelled its members—Burnham, McKim, Olmsted Jr., and Saint-Gaudens. With the exception of Saint-Gaudens, who was unwell, the commission began its enterprise with a seven-week tour of great European cities, paying particular attention to the sites that had influenced L'Enfant in his original design—particularly Paris and Versailles. L'Enfant had spent childhood years at Versailles, where his father was a decorative painter, and was familiar with the garden designs of Louis XIV's landscape architect, André Lenôtre. Senator McMillan's aide, Charles Moore, served

as the group's notetaker and organizer and, along with Olmsted Jr., drafted the final plan. Some years later Moore would write biographies of Burnham and McKim and would chair for years the Commission of Fine Arts as it guided the implementation of the McMillan Plan. Charles Moore was another point of continuity in Washington's beautification.

Up until the eleventh hour, hands were frantically at work to complete the exhibition of the McMillan Commission's plan for Washington. Lore has it that as President Theodore Roosevelt walked in one door to inspect the presentation, trash and materials were being hustled out another door by those who had labored all night on the models. For the many creative people who had worked so hard and brilliantly, not to mention politically—Burnham, for one, had negotiated removal of the Pennsylvania Railroad from the Mall to a future Union Station he would design—public enthusiasm for the plan was an enormous reward. (The commission's models and many of their drawings have been preserved. The models were transferred to the Smithsonian Institution, and the drawings remain in the collection of the Commission of Fine Arts.)

Although the plan for Washington met with widespread approval and many of its features were later implemented, including the Lincoln Memorial, reflecting pool, Memorial Bridge, and Union

Station, political infighting immediately set in, preventing action for years. Creating the Commission of Fine Arts in 1910, among whose first members were Olmsted Jr. and Charles Moore, started the process of implementing the plan. Seven years later, Olmsted Jr.'s firm—Olmsted Brothers—was contracted to study Rock Creek Park, resulting in the Report of 1918. Then, in the 1940s, Rock Creek Park administrators contacted Olmsted Jr. for an updated opinion on the park's vegetation management, to which he responded with a four-page report.

The timing, tenacious and ingenious leadership, and intricate connections associated with the McMillan Plan's success, and its significance to Washington's monumental core, admired the world over today, make this episode in American history and politics not only memorable but thrilling. It is a nugget, mostly forgotten, but one that had enormous and lasting impact.[10]

3 | The Olmsteds

Frederick Law Olmsted Jr. (1870–1957) left a deep imprint on the nation's capital city—on both its monumental core and its parks. Although not all of his park goals reached fruition, his principles for the ideal cityscape have endured. Like his father, he was a brilliant workhorse whose career spanned half a century. Olmsted Sr., a longtime bachelor who had tried out several careers before settling down, married his brother John's widow, Mary Cleveland Perkins, several years after John died of tuberculosis. He became stepfather to his young nephews, John Charles and Owen, and niece, Charlotte. The couple had two sons before Frederick Jr. was born, but these children died in infancy and at childbirth. The Olmsteds also had a daughter, Marion, who was nine when Frederick Jr. was born on July 24, 1870, on Staten Island, New York, where the family lived at the time. John Charles was eighteen, Charlotte, fifteen, and Owen, thirteen. Named Henry Perkins Olmsted at birth, Olmsted Jr. underwent a name change in early childhood to become his father's namesake and was thereafter called Rick. His father, whose fame in landscape architecture—a field he turned into a legitimate profession in the United States—had begun to peak, wanted his

only biological son to carry forth his legacy, not only in landscape architecture but also into its nascent offshoots, city planning and national parks. Olmsted Jr.'s indelible imprint on Washington, D.C., was but the first achievement of a long career—he was thirty-one when he joined the McMillan Commission—and stands as the best representation of his father's traditions. So much spun into motion after that, as other American cities solicited the younger Olmsted's expertise. His early career quickly broadened to fully encompass urban planning, which became his own sphere. He was a founding member and president of the National Conference on City Planning and the American City Planning Institute. He and his half-brother John Charles founded the American Society of Landscape Architects and also served as its presidents at various times. From 1900 to 1915, Olmsted Jr. taught at Harvard's landscape architecture school, having inaugurated the program; he soon became the Charles Eliot Professor of Landscape Architecture. (Charles Eliot, whose father was a president of Harvard University, had been a partner in the Olmsted firm from 1893 to 1897, until his premature death at age 38.) In the early decades of the twentieth century

Countless future Americans will unknowingly pay tribute to Frederick Law Olmsted [Jr.]— when, in visiting a great national or state park, they exclaim, "This is a place of great beauty— how fortunate it has been preserved for us."

—Newton B. Drury, Director, National Park Service, 1929–1940 [11]

Frederick Law Olmsted Jr. Courtesy of the National Park Service, Frederick Law Olmsted National Historic Site.

Olmsted Jr. solidified his contribution to the city planning field and, as his father had done with landscape architecture, made it a legitimate profession. Of his Washington phase and contributions, Charles Moore wrote of Olmsted:

> *Frederick Law Olmsted as a member of the Senate Park Commission was responsible for laying out the District outer park system. His shoe-prints marked every hill and valley within the remaining Seven Mile Square, regions often as primitive as Ellicott [L'Enfant's surveyor] found them in 1792. Now he was taking up the task of carrying out park plans of his own devising.... A tremendous worker, a sound scholar in both history and example, an exuberant, boyish, engaging personality, he had L'Enfant's way of "seeing things in the large."* [12]

There is no doubt that Olmsted thrived during this early part of his career, of which much time went to city plan-

ning, his more famous commissions being Boulder, Pittsburgh, New Haven, and Rochester. Baltimore's Roland Park, Forest Hills Gardens in Queens, and Palos Verdes Estates on California's coast were several of his important community developments. Soon after the elder Olmsted retired from Olmsted, Olmsted, and Eliot in 1895, and his partner, Charles Eliot, suddenly died in 1897, Olmsted Jr. and his brother John Charles became partners, renaming the business the Olmsted Brothers. Over the course of nearly a century (1857–1950), the family firm designed thousands of landscape projects, including more than two hundred schools and college campuses, 650 parks and recreation areas, and more than nine hundred private estates. Olmsted Jr. was avidly involved in all categories of the firm's projects, and yet any assessment of his career and the man himself distills down to one theme that was his personal passion and largest success in life: the creation and preservation of national and state parks. He involved himself in establishing the National Park Service in 1916 and crafted some of the legislation's language, including this statement of the new bureau's purpose: "to conserve the scenery and the natural and historic objects and the wild life therein and to provide for the enjoyment of same in such manner and by such means as will leave them unimpaired for the enjoyment of future generations." [13]

More than any other individual, Olmsted Jr. was behind the creation of the California State Park System. And there, as in Washington, D.C., an "Olmsted Report" became a vital and enduring document:

The California State Park Survey of 1928, commonly referred to as the Olmsted Report, was the Magna Charta of the California State Park System. His original report, supplemented by him in 1945 ... has been followed with remarkable fidelity. It is a profound discussion of principles that are as sound today as they were thirty years ago. [14]

It may be true that Olmsted Sr. was a commissioner and advocate of Yosemite before it became a national park, but his son's involvement was on another, more visceral and eternal level. Olmsted Jr. wrote in 1921, following a two-month journey to national parks and forests:

Beyond all the interesting natural objects and activities, animal, vegetable, and geological; beyond all the opportunities for healthful, joyous exercise; beyond all the beauty of each landscape that I saw, no matter how impressive or beautiful; the one thing which made the deepest impression on me and which I believe to be the most priceless recreational quality of these great reservations was the sense of freedom and independence which they give. To be free, and to know that one is free, of his own right as human being, with-

out trespass or intrusion, to go where the spirit moves, up hill or down dale, in any direction, day after day, unfenced, unhedged, untrammeled by the vexing artificial web of property rights and other restrictions on personal liberty which a crowded civilization has built to keep its close-packed life from chaos, does more than anything else to calm the nerves and cool the temper and rest the mind of the ordinary modern civilized man, harassed by his struggles in that web grown too complex for him to understand and accept in its entirety as reasonable. [15]

Involved in the planning for many national and state parks and a consultant to the Park Service for years, Olmsted also provided early leadership in California's Save-the-Redwoods League; his role was of such importance that a grove in Prairie Creek Redwoods State Park is named for him. At the Olmsted Grove's dedication on Olmsted's eighty-third birthday in 1953, the world's leading "park man" accepted the honor with these words:

In so far as I deserve this great honor I think it [is] because, in dealing with existing real landscapes, I have been guided by an injunction impressed on me by my distinguished father: namely, that when one becomes responsible for what is to happen to such a landscape his prime duty is to protect and perpetuate whatever of beauty and inspirational value, inherent in that land-

scape, is due to nature and to circumstances not of one's own contriving, and to humbly subordinate to that purpose any impulse to exercise upon it one's own skill as a creative designer. [16]

It could not have been easy being the son of a distinguished and authoritative father, and yet Olmsted and his half-brother John Charles avidly pursued successful, individually rewarding careers that also carried on the family tradition, with which their father, in his late years, had become obsessed, partly because of his declining mental health. One aspect of Olmsted Sr.'s obsession was that his son Rick gain the proper education that he himself had lacked. Rick fulfilled this dream by graduating from Harvard in 1894 and apprenticing in several landscape disciplines, including horticulture and forestry on George Vanderbilt's Biltmore Estate in North Carolina, the elder Olmsted's final, grand-scale project. The father bore down relentlessly on his namesake:

*You must, with the aid of such inheritance as I can give you, make good on my failings.... Therefore look sharp to benefit by that in which you have special opportunities to bene-fit at Biltmore. There are many requirements of your profession which can be provided elsewhere. Your school for nearly all wisdom in trees and plants and planting is at Biltmore.... Review! Review and **train** yourself.*

And in another letter father admonished son:

*I shall not take you into this office until you are much better grounded in trees and shrubs than anyone here now except Manning. If you think it is impracticable, the sooner you give up the profession the better. But I know it is **not impracticable** and I **insist** on your making yourself an expert nursery man.* [17]

That father and son had a symbiotic relationship is apparent. Olmsted Sr.'s overbearing qualities, demonstrated in his prolific correspondence to his son as the latter reached maturity, were tempered with unconditional love that helped to balance the relationship. Olmsted Jr.'s humble, collaborative, and public-service-oriented personality also must have contributed to the unusual parent-child fusion. By the time Olmsted Jr. was in his mid-twenties, his father's active life was over, although he lived another seven years in a mentally impaired state; thus Olmsted Jr. gained complete independence as a young man.

This story of Rock Creek Park and the Olmsted Report of 1918 honors the great and lasting contribution of Frederick Law Olmsted Jr. to his country's landscapes, rural and urban. We know from his writings that he had a deep and sagacious

Frederick Law Olmsted, father of landscape architecture in the United States.

Opposite: John Charles Olmsted, son of Frederick Law Olmsted's wife, Mary, from her first marriage to Olmsted's half-brother John, who died prematurely. Courtesy of the National Park Service, Frederick Law Olmsted National Historic Site.

Frederick Law Olmsted (1822–1903)

Frederick Law Olmsted achieved fame in his lifetime. He was a genius, with vision and ideals that his tremendous energy and workaholic habits brought to fruition time and again. He was a leader, a reformer, a man of action, a creator, and had the power to steer a larger society in the direction he thought was correct. He impacted the world around him, was respected for doing so, and shaped social and civic attitudes that remain part of American culture today. Although his sons went on to produce landscape projects that far surpassed in number his own creations, the eldest Olmsted, the father of American landscape architecture, pioneered every prospect he undertook to explore, from his travels through the South to study slavery, to his partnership in the enlightened *Putnam's Monthly* magazine, to his design with Calvert Vaux for Central Park, to his Civil War directorship of the U.S. Sanitary Commission, to his management of the Mariposa gold-mining estate in California, to his advocacy for national parks. He was visible to all, leading, planning, creating, crusading, reforming, networking, laying foundations, and always writing. While accomplishing so much, he also valued family, friends, and colleagues and consciously 'sought quality experiences with all of them. He is largely forgotten today, although many cities are restoring his and his children's legacies to

mind, and we know from the chronology of his accomplishments that he channeled every fiber of his gifts toward the improvement of our civilization through practical and aesthetic planning and through conservation. As one of his eulogizers wrote shortly after his death in 1957, "It certainly may be said of Frederick Law Olmsted, as of the great architect, Sir Christopher Wren, 'If you seek his monument, look about you.'" [18]

our culture and ideals. His most famous works, which often took years to complete, include Central Park (1858); Brooklyn's Prospect Park (1866); Buffalo's park system (1868); Chicago's South Parks (1871); Illinois's Riverside residential community (1868); Montreal's Mount Royale Park (1874); Detroit's Belle Isle Park (1881); the U.S. Capitol grounds (1874); the campuses of Lawrenceville School (1883) and Stanford University (1886); the Biltmore estate (1891); and the World's Columbian Exposition (1893). [19]

John Charles Olmsted (1852–1920)
Well versed in his stepfather's landscape principles and paternalism, John Charles Olmsted bowed to the yoke of family business after a brief youthful rebellion when he dreamt of becoming an architect. "You are not a man of genius in art," the great patriarch admonished his stepson in a long letter in 1877. "A man of less artistic impulse I never knew…. Consequently as you have insisted on making yourself an artist, you must spend great labor, years of study with little satisfaction of any worthy ambition." [20] What the elder Olmsted had counted on was not only a partner in his flourishing business but also the establishment of Olmsted patrimony in the field of landscape architecture that he had defined: "The chances of the good will of my business, when I am dead or superannuated, to any one capable of making it amica-

ble, are equivalent in value to a moderate fortune … worth more than all else I can leave my family." [21] If Olmsted's behavior toward his children seems coercive by contemporary standards, probably his children viewed it as both typical parental authority of the day, when family businesses often lasted generations, and also as a reaction to their father's own less-directed youth, when he would have appreciated greater parental guidance. He often repeated in his letters that he did not want his children to

make the same mistakes he had made—a
universal desire in parents.

Thus John Olmsted entered the family
business early and became a full partner in
1884 when the firm moved permanently
to Brookline, Massachusetts. He proved a
talented and prolific designer in addition
to being an astute manager. His major
projects included park systems for Dayton,
Ohio; Seattle and Spokane, Washington;
Fall River, Massachusetts; Portland,
Oregon; and Portland, Maine. Besides con-
tributing to Boston's Emerald Necklace, he
designed city parks in Charleston and
New Orleans and fulfilled hundreds of
commissions to design landscapes for
schools, universities, libraries, state capitols,
and other institutions and municipal buildings. With his half-brother he founded and
served as president of the American
Society of Landscape Architects. Under
John's stewardship, the family business
more than tripled its number of projects.

Photograph by
"Thompson," 1945.
Courtesy of the
Washingtoniana Division,
D.C. Public Library.

4 | Rock Creek Park Report of 1918

In 1917, Frederick Law Olmsted Jr., the nation's leading landscape architect and a celebrated Washington, D.C., planner, was the natural choice to make a study of Rock Creek Park and offer suggestions for its management. He already knew the park intimately, having served, in 1901, on the eminent U.S. Senate Park Commission, (McMillan Commission), which produced, the following year, the blueprint for Washington, D.C.'s public buildings and regional park system, and for which Olmsted was responsible for the park-system portion. As it took decades to implement significant portions of the McMillan Plan, which paid respect to Pierre Charles L' Enfant's original design of 1791, it is not surprising that planning for Rock Creek Park, of lower priority to city planners, came as late as 1917. Sadly, lack of sufficient funds, a problem that persists today, left much of the inspired Olmsted plan unrealized. Fortunately, the values articulated in the report have endured, and the document has served as a canon for park administrators since it first appeared. Olmsted Jr.'s principles for a city park carried on his father's tradition: to create a usable public space for all citizens to enjoy while at the same time preserving the natural scenery. To achieve this end,

roads, paths, bridges, and selected structures were a necessity, but their presence had to appear subordinate to the landscape.

The Rock Creek Park Report, whose foreword is on page 33, divided the park into six divisions according to landscape features: valley, plateau recreation ground, woodland, open hillside, wilder woodland, and meadow. Within each landscape division, plantings were identified by type— natural forest, open woodland, bushy hilltop growth, and open grassland—and a program for their maintenance or restoration was offered. The report also provided advice on the construction of roads, thoroughfare crossings, bridges, paths, fences, and buildings within the park, and made suggestions for boundary improvements.

Excerpts of the Olmsted Report (page 35) follow the order of the original report and reveal a thrilling continuity in the park's purpose, unique natural features, and scenic beauty. The park and the Olmsted Report have endured; yet, as the metropolitan area continues to grow feverishly, with grave endangerment to the environment, only increased public consciousness and activism about the park's vulnerability will safeguard its future as a precious wilderness in the middle of urban turbulence. [22]

There is no doubt that the enjoyment of beautiful natural scenery is to the majority of city dwellers one of the most refreshing antidotes for the wearing influences of city life.

—Frederick Law Olmsted Jr.

ROCK CREEK PARK

A report by

OLMSTED BROTHERS

December 1918

FOREWORD

The dominant consideration, never to be subordinated to any other purpose in dealing with Rock Creek Park, is the permanent preservation of its wonderful natural beauty, and the making of that beauty accessible to the people without spoiling the scenery in the process.

Its preservation differs radically from the protection of any unchanging thing of beauty in a museum in that it involves an unending watchful struggle to neutralize destructive forces inevitably acting on the scenery; to reinforce and supplement its natural powers of resistance and recuperation: and patiently, skillfully, and humbly to restore the actual deterioration. The scenery of the Park cannot remain absolutely static: it is always changing for better or for worse: in many respects it has for years been deteriorating. The great problem of its management is to convert progressive deterioration into progressive restoration.

To clarify understanding of these basic principles, and to point out as far as possible appropriate ways and means of applying them is the prime endeavor of this report.

Opposite: Photograph from the Rock Creek Park Report of 1918, with caption: "A delightful glimpse of the creek with its rocks and its overhanging foliage. Many such glimpses are now blocked by foliage which could be removed without essential change in the character of the stream's surroundings." Courtesy of the National Park Service, Frederick Law Olmsted National Historic Site. 2837-47

Rock Creek Park Report of 1918, photograph © 2002 Herman Woerner. Courtesy of the National Park Service, Frederick Law Olmsted National Historic Site.

Afternoon in the Woods,
by "Horace," 1905.
Courtesy of the
Washingtoniana Division,
D.C. Public Library.

The Justifying Value of the Park

It is unnecessary to praise the very excep-
tional natural beauty of Rock Creek Park,
because it is well known and widely
appreciated. But it is important to empha-
size the fact that it is upon the subtle
qualities of this essentially wild and natural beauty that the public value of the
Park is unquestionably found in the recreative value of its natural qualities—large
stretches of forest, the river valley, dark
ravines, steep and rolling hills, and occasional meadow lands—and no use or
exploitation or development of any sort
can ever be right that is not based upon
this fundamental conception.... But no
matter how perfect the scenery of the
Park may be or may become, no matter
how high its potential value, that value
remains potential except insofar as it is
enjoyed by large and ever larger numbers
of people, poor and rich alike.

[There are] three fundamental consid-
erations in accordance with which the
Park must be developed.... *First,* its interesting, varied, natural scenery must be
saved intact insofar as possible, must in
some respects be restored or perfected by
intelligent, appreciative landscape development, and must not be replaced by other
and more or less foreign types of "treat-

ment." *Second,* the Park must be opened
up to the driving, riding, and walking
public; but the roads, paths, and other
accompaniments of intensive use must be
so located and so built that the essential
qualities of the Park are impaired in the
least possible degree. *Third,* adequate trans-
portation must be provided to and into
the Park for people dependent upon street
car service.

Analysis of Scenery

What is the innate character of this natural
landscape? What are those subtle qualities
which give it a beauty so distinctive and
so precious? Definition and analysis are
not easy. Nevertheless it is a clear appreciation and understanding of those very
qualities that must now and for all time
guide the maintenance and development
of the Park....

The land forms of Rock Creek Valley
... are of considerable variety. Here the
valley is narrow and gorge-like, with rocky
forest-clad sides dropping abruptly to the
Creek which breaks and tumbles along
over a stoney bed. Here the enclosing hillsides fall back and become less steep and
rugged, the stream flows more slowly and
quietly between overarching trees through
a broader and more peaceful valley with

an occasional open hillside or a bit of grassy meadow. The scenery becomes more restful and more simple in its beauty. Again there is the contrast of bold picturesqueness on one side and gentle slopes or open fields on the other. These types of scenery are found in endless variety and beauty of form and detail: they vary with every point of view and again with every season of the year and every hour of the day. Best of all they are pictures within the Park—the everchanging landscape of a winding river valley and its tributaries, enclosed and guarded by the forest-covered hills on either side. This is the larger scenery of the Park.

The other is that more intimate and smaller scenery.... Rugged gray ledges softened with moss and contrasted with picturesque groups of Kalmia; a gnarly old plane tree or group of hornbeams or of river birches overhanging the water; the moist bank of a dark wooded ravine carpeted with ferns; the spreading oak in the open field; the crooked form of a dogwood arching over a woodland trail; the sudden accents of the cedars and their pleasing combinations of color and form with sumac and sassafras and scrubby ground covers; and most important of all, the everchanging picture as one wanders through the forest: the forms and groupings of tree trunks, the variety and intricate detail of the undergrowth of woodland shrubs and young trees, and the

delicate forms and infinite variety of the ferns, mosses, creeping vines and woodland flowers, the natural ground cover of the forest—these make the more intimate scenery of the Rock Creek valley.

These two sorts of scenery are not peculiar to Rock Creek Park, but in this beautiful valley with its many ramifications they are found in a high degree of perfection and in almost unlimited variety. It is the extraordinary combination of this circumstance with the proximity of the valley to a great city that gives to the Park its unique value. This is the value which was first preserved by Act of Congress for the benefit of all people. It is now and always will be the only value that can justify the maintenance of this great natural park.

Primary Landscape and Administrative Divisions
Division A: Valley Section. This is topographically and psychologically the backbone, as it were, of the Park, and it would be a great misfortune if any use should develop that would to the least appreciable degree injure the present charm and beauty of this valley scenery. Rock Creek Valley with its main tributaries—Piney Branch and Broad Branch valleys and the valley of Military Road—forms an arterial system of most beautiful valley scenes or landscapes. This self-contained scenery has great variety and at the same time a happy unity of character. Its linear quality too

Plan No. 29, Rock Creek Report of 1918. Courtesy of the National Park Service, Frederick Law Olmsted National Historic Site.

adds to its charm by ever stimulating the desire to explore beyond the next turn. It is this conception—beautiful, varying, self-contained valley scenery—which should be paramount in controlling the development and use of Division A. Picnic groves by the creek, wading pools and the like are entirely permissible and desirable, for the water is a great drawing card for the public; but such uses should always and unmistakably be incidental. Swimming holes, for instance, should probably not be permitted, for they inevitably require toilet and dressing rooms, and in some cases screens from the drive, all of which work distinct injury to the beauty of the valley scenery; while at best these "holes" can provide only inferior accommodations for swimming.

Division B: Plateau Recreation Ground.

Division B is a section of plateau land separated topographically from the rest of the Park, easily accessible from adjacent residential areas and, by car, from other parts of the District. It is admirably adapted for more or less intensive recreation—tennis, basket ball, cricket, football, and band concerts—and has already been tentatively allotted for this purpose.

Division C: Woodland for Intensive Use.

Division C, an area of about three hundred acres, is primarily a forest unit. Topographically it is roughly of

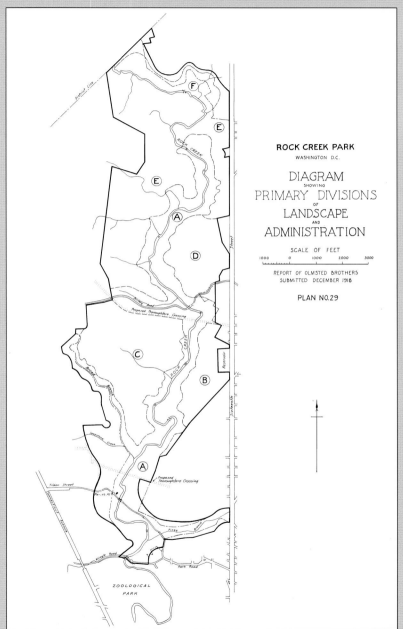

ROCK CREEK PARK
WASHINGTON D.C.

DIAGRAM
SHOWING
PRIMARY DIVISIONS
OF
LANDSCAPE
AND
ADMINISTRATION

SCALE OF FEET

REPORT OF OLMSTED BROTHERS
SUBMITTED DECEMBER 1918

PLAN NO.29

the plateau type, but it is generally rolling and is intersected with several sharp ravines leading down to Rock Creek and furnishing added variety and interest for the recreation seeker. In addition to possessing many of the recreative elements to be found in a woodland park of this sort, the area is particularly well adapted for exploration and enjoyment by pedestrians, for it is much less subdivided into abrupt hills and valleys than most parts of the Park, avoiding thus the constant expenditure of effort not often appreciated or desired by people not looking primarily for exercise. Lastly, but of fundamental importance, is the question of accessibility. Assuming a thoroughfare with car line crossing the Park probably along the ridge immediately south of the Military Road (to be discussed later), area "C" becomes ideally accessible....

Roads and bridle paths should be minimized, and there should be many picnic groves, springs, unobtrusive seats, summer houses, and other local objectives of interest. The spaces free from undergrowth ... should be large and frequent enough to encourage and accommodate a more or less unrestricted movement of people about the woodlands regardless of fixed paths.

Division D: Open Hillside Section.
Division D, about 150 acres, is primarily a unit of open land. It has an interesting topography of rolling hills; and it affords a sense of freedom, breadth, and outlook found nowhere else in the Park.... It is old farm land, in parts overgrown with scrub pine and more or less cut up by hedgerows—not now very attractive. And yet by some cutting of hedgerows and pines and by a little careful planting we believe it can be made beautiful and interesting. Because of its quality of openness it possesses a recreative value so different from that of other parts of the Park that no use or development in any way detracting from that quality should be permitted. For instance the arboretum which has been started here would, if allowed to remain, tend to defeat this very quality.... An arboretum would be an exotic element, and hence a very undesirable one....

A free use by all classes of patrons whether riding, driving, or walking should be encouraged insofar as this can be done without materially marring the simple breadth and beauty of its grassy slopes, and the great charm of the varying landscape as seen from these slopes and hilltops. Occasional groups and specimens of trees are needed for shade and landscape effect; walks on easy grades, occasional unobtrusive seats, groves or simple overlook terraces at points of commanding outlook, and such roads and bridle paths as are required to reveal the beauty of the landscape—these are needed. Further than that, simple rolling pasture or mowed grass-land should prevail. Few defined walks will be needed, as pedestrians should be encouraged to spread over the turf at will.

Division E: Wilder Woodland. The bulk of this area—some 450 acres—... is a forest area, and the wild natural character of its forests should be preserved to the highest degree.... and the preservation of the finer details of the natural woodland scenery requires that pedestrians be more or less restricted to the walks and other defined ways. Some picnic grounds and other objects of local interest will be needed ... but essentially this division should be one where the wildness of the forest will be enjoyed from the paths, roads, and bridle paths, and shall remain unmarred by the wear and tear largely unavoidable in areas of more intensive use, such as Divisions B, C, and D....

It would be clear folly to allow the sum total of park value to deteriorate for want of a little regulation that would insure ultimately a far higher degree of service to the public as a whole—the owners of the Park.

Division F: Meadow Park. It is, or is proposed to be, an irregular stretch of flat meadow land some four thousand feet long, varying from two hundred to eight hundred or nine hundred feet in width. Its value as a landscape unit, enclosed by woods, interesting in form and entirely self-contained, is very great and, in this park, unique.... [I]t should be defended jealously against any inharmonious encroachments upon the simplicity, breadth, and restfulness inherent in its very character. But any use of the meadow should be welcomed which does not disturb the simple broad stretch of greensward.

Regarding a National Arboretum and Botanic Garden in Rock Creek Park. It seems best here to give attention to the proposition often put forward, to use the northern part of Rock Creek Park for a National Arboretum and Botanic Garden. The idea is in its very essence so full of danger to the fundamental purposes of the Park, that we take the liberty of quoting at length the arguments as set forth by the Commission of Fine Arts in their Report to the Committee on the Library, House of Representatives, U.S., dated September 18, 1917.

If the Botanic Garden is established in Rock Creek Park the inevitable result will be the gradual frittering away of a priceless and self-consistent piece of natural scenery.... this piece of ground was set apart by Congress for the preservation of its natural scenery.

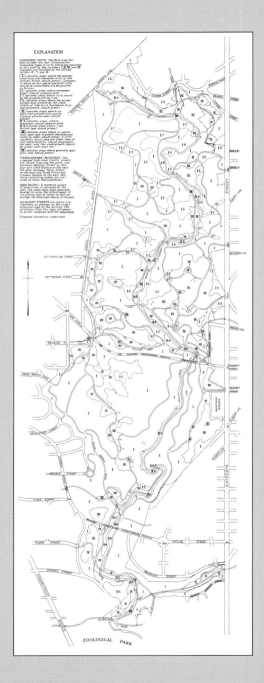

ROCK CREEK PARK
WASHINGTON · D.C.
DIAGRAMATIC PLAN FOR LANDSCAPE UNITS
SHOWING ALSO
PROPOSED TRAFFIC THOROUGHFARES ACROSS THE PARK
AND A SYSTEM OF PARK DRIVES

SCALE OF FEET

TO ACCOMPANY THE REPORT OF
OLMSTED BROTHERS · LANDSCAPE ARCHITECTS
DECEMBER 1918

PLAN No. 27

Plan No. 27, Rock
Creek Report of 1918.
Courtesy of the National
Park Service, Frederick
Law Olmsted National
Historic Site.

Legend from Plan No. 27 *(at left)*

Explanation

Landscape Units—The Park area has been divided into four fundamental landscape types or units which are indicated on this plan by the numbers I, II, III, and IV. Subtypes are indicated by the affixed letters -E, -T, and -R.

I indicates areas where the general conditions and characteristics of the natural forest should prevail. Subtypes, in which certain special characteristics should be encouraged, are designated as follows:

I-E indicates areas where evergreen forest should predominate.

I-T indicates areas where tulip should be the predominating tree.

I-R indicates areas where the normal bottom land growth by the creek chiefly of river birch, hornbeam tulip and sycamore should prevail.

II indicates areas where an open tree growth with usually a grassy ground cover should prevail.

II-E indicates areas where evergreen should predominate.

II-R indicates areas where river bottom type should prevail.

III indicates areas where an upland semi-open type of growth characterized chiefly by cedar, should prevail. A little sassafras, locust, pine and other trees of like characteristics should accompany the cedar; and the undergrowth should be sumac, wild roses, etc.

IV indicates areas where generally open grass land should prevail.

Thoroughfare Crossings—Two proposed high-level traffic streets are shown crossing the park, one between Madison Street on the east and Utah Avenue on the west, the other between Taylor Street on the east and Yuma Street and Linnean on the west. Tentative controlling grades are indicated on these thoroughfares.

Park Drives—A tentative system of park drives is indicated on the plan. The roads have been generally located to serve the future needs of circulation and to reveal to best advantage the landscape beauty of the park.

Adjacent Streets are shown substantially as planned on the street extension map of the District. The variations from this map will appear on prints combined with the topography.

Proposed elevations underlined.

Suggestions Relating to the Creation and Maintenance of Landscape Types

It is out of the question to depend upon written directions for detailed guidance in landscape forestry work of this sort, for after the general aims and methods have been determined comes the delicate and very important work of fitting these methods to the local detailed conditions as they exist. And this can be done only on the spot. In other words, the success of this sort of work must ultimately depend upon a thorough appreciation and understanding, on the part of those actually directing the work, of the essential character and quality of the effects sought after. Slight variations in the matter of doing the work, variations due even to the differing judgements of skilled men, are liable to make such immense differences in the quality of the results that a one-man control of this work seems a distinctly wise policy.... Every year as long as the Park is kept up, must call for a careful, intelligent, appreciative and above all *consistent* maintenance of the landscape details.

Construction in the Park

It may not be out of place here to offer a word or two of caution and suggestions regarding buildings, bridges, seats, fences, and other park structures, as well as roads, bridle paths, and footways. A building of inharmonious, self-assertive design is apt to inflict almost incalculable injury upon the natural beauty of the scenery within which it is placed. This is obviously true if the self-assertive object be of inferior artistic quality in itself; but it is no less true of an object which in itself may have great artistic merit so long as that object distracts attention from the beauty of the landscape. This applies in varying degree to all park structures of whatever kind and size. They should be so designed and

located as to fall naturally into place as part and parcel of the scenery, and should never stand out as objects complete in themselves with the surrounding landscape becoming merely a background. The split rail fences along the roadsides and many of the foot-bridges now found in the Park are happy examples of this fitness of design.

The roads, bridle paths, and especially the footways ... should always and unmistakably fit into the landscape as harmonious and subordinate parts of the scenery through which they pass. Like other park construction they are primarily a means to an end—they merely enable the people to enjoy the refreshing beauty of the park scenery. If in the process they inflict injury upon that scenery or distract attention from it to their own assertive qualities, by just so much do they fail of their primary purpose.

These "ways" of travel, therefore, should first of all exhibit to the maximum the beauty and variety and charm of the scenery. Next, and no less important, they should be so planned and studied in detail as to "seem to belong" where they are. In the case of roads their lines and grades should harmonize with the major lines and forms of the scenery through which they pass; they are seldom beautiful in themselves, wherefore it is doubly important that they take a congruous and subordinate place in the landscape. In the case of bridle and foot paths, they should be adjusted carefully and without apparent effort to existing rock formations, to the trees and tree groups, to the courses of brooks, to interesting groups of shrubs and other wild plants, in fact to the thousand and one details which make up the intricate beauty of the woodland scenery or the simpler beauty of the more open landscapes. Because people travel slowly along the foot paths—and often along the bridle paths—they have opportunity to see and to appreciate these countless smaller details of beauty and fitness.… In locating paths, therefore, effort must always be exerted to make them inviting, to lead the pleasure-seeker along with the minimum of mental and physical effort on his part, to avoid steep grades and unnecessary ups and downs much more generally than has been done in the paths thus far opened, and to avoid indirect and circuitous lines except where they are apparently the lines of least resistance.

As the Park develops, these many and various artificial elements must of necessity increase; and the more numerous they become the greater is the danger of serious injury to the landscape of the Park.

Rectification of Park Boundaries
The fundamental reason for rectification of boundaries—which usually means more takings—is the preservation of park scenery from intruding private property development.… Adjustments are indicated on the accompanying diagram No. 30.…

Thoroughfare Crossings
There are two main requirements to be borne in mind: first, to carry the traffic across the Park in that manner and in that location which will obtrude least into the natural landscape; and second, to locate the thoroughfares so that the car lines may give the maximum of service as approaches to and into the Park.

Conclusion
In general we would not urge a sudden and large expansion of activities and "improvements"; for it is conceivable that the Park development might easily be carried too fast and too far. The inherent value of the naturalistic "undeveloped" qualities of this Park cannot be overestimated. For in those qualities lies the essential justification for all that has been done and spent, for all that will be done and spent to give this great Park to the people. In its *development* the guiding policy should be distinctly one of restraint; in its *maintenance* the policy should be liberal, in order to meet the continuously increasing needs of the patrons and still more to protect and insure the permanent values of a great public investment.

Photograph from the Rock Creek Park Report of 1918. Courtesy of the National Park Service, Frederick Law Olmsted National Historic Site. 2837-46

PART OF THE
OTHER
PICNIC
ROCK CREEK PARK, MAY 18 1918   S T D & ME

In early 1922, Olmsted Jr. sent gynecologist and renaissance man Robert Latou Dickinson (1861–1950) a copy of the Rock Creek Park Report of 1918 for Dickinson's proposed "Washington Walk Book." The book was never completed, and in 1942 Dickinson donated the unpublished notebook of sketches, watercolors, and photographs to the Library of Congress, along with rough drafts for the tour guide. The chapter on Rock Creek Park quoted long passages from the Olmsted Report.

Rock Creek Park is a very personal park. You, yourself, really discovered it. Even though someone may have led you to it. The very name flashes pictures on your screen. One such flash is the autumn woods in full color in the late afternoon when, happily lost on a vanishing trail, on a down-dropping ridge, you lingered dreaming, to listen to the murmuring river beneath, and the dust overtook you and the light failed....

The next picture to leap into color is that of the hot noon when, tired by clambering over one hillside after another, you stopped abruptly out of dim forest tangle on to the brilliant still green meadow, with the willows trailing in the mirror above the dam. That was the first day you lunched at the Mill....

Or, last of all, that morning in Springtime, when gazing through the delicate mist, up at the two bridges hung high in the sky, on a turn in the roadway, there, on a bench in the banked blooming laurel,—all of a sudden—Herself. It is a very personal Park.

—Robert L. Dickinson,
"Washington Walk Book," 1918

Chronology:
Park Administration and Structures

1890   For the first forty-three years, Rock Creek Park was under military supervision. The Rock Creek Park Commission included the Army chief of engineers, Brig. Gen. Thomas L. Casey, who was also chairman; the engineer commissioner of the District of Columbia, Lt. Col. Henry M. Rober; and three presidential appointees—Brig. Gen. Henry V. Boynton, R. Ross Perry, and Prof. Samuel P. Langley, secretary of the Smithsonian Institution. The commission's executive officer, Capt. William T. Rossell, was the assistant to the District engineer commissioner and also served as the commission's executive officer. He was succeeded two years later by Capt. Gustav J. Fieberger. Over the next few years, this commission acquired 1,605.976 acres of land for the park and then ceased its active role in park affairs. The park's additional acreage was acquired at different times and tended to include tributary stream valleys, such as Piney Branch and Soapstone valleys.

1894   A Board of Control had been legislated to administer the park, and it represented the D.C. commissioners and the Army chief of engineers. The District engineer commissioner served on the board (in addition to serving on the park commission) and his assistant, Capt. Gustav J. Fieberger, who was also the executive officer on the park commission, served as secretary and was the first de facto superintendent of Rock Creek Park.

1896   Capt. Lansing H. Beach succeeded Fieberger and remained secretary of the board even after advancing to the position of District engineer commissioner. In 1901, Beach Drive was named for him in honor of his dedication to the park.

1907   Lee R. Grabill, a civilian assistant to Beach, assumed the park's managerial role, while at the same time overseeing District roads. By 1916, he was referred to as superintendent of Rock Creek Park.

1912   The Joaquin Miller Cabin was dismantled and moved to the park to commemorate the California poet Cincinnatus H. Miller (nicknamed Joaquin), who had built the cabin in 1883 off of Sixteenth Street.

Rock Creek, 2001, by Barbara Nuss, oil on linen, 20 x 27 in. Courtesy of the artist.

1918 In September, Congress made Rock Creek Park part of the District's park system. Supervisory powers were transferred from the Board of Control to the District's Office of Public Buildings and Grounds, with Col. Clarence Ridley reporting to the Army chief of engineers. The Office of Public Buildings and Grounds had been supervising District parks since 1867.

Grabill, on the staff of the District's engineer commissioner, became separated from the park, but his staff of three skilled laborers, a wagon boss, nine unskilled workers, and one foreman, Patrick Joyce, remained.

The civilian superintendent of the Office of Public Buildings and Grounds under Ridley was Francis F. Gillen. He supervised Joyce, Joyce's staff, and a professional forester who came on board in 1920. Gillen played a leading role in park management until the 1940s.

1919 Rock Creek Board was established in February after the Commission of Fine Arts, created in 1910, approved the Olmsted Report, and Col. Ridley's office undertook to implement it. Two staff landscape architects were assigned to study the report, recommend improvements, and report on work carried out. The Commission of Fine Arts landscape architect, James L. Greenleaf, who had succeeded Olmsted in 1918, wrote letters to the commission's chairman, Charles Moore, stating that in his opinion, Ridley was not up to the task of implementing the report.

1921 Lt. Col. Clarence O. Sherrill replaced Col. Ridley as officer in charge in March 1921. Greenleaf urged him to study the Olmsted Report in order to check the serious damage being done.

1925 In February, an Act of Congress abolished the Office of Public Buildings and Grounds under the Army chief of engineers and turned over its functions to a newly created Office of Public Buildings and Public Parks of the National Capital. Sherrill assumed directorship of the successor agency and reported to the president. Sherrill set the wheels in motion for Maryland to acquire land that would extend Rock Creek Park beyond the District line. Federal appropriations aided this effort, and by 1930 work was well under way for the Maryland portion of the park, which ultimately encompassed 4,193 acres and stretched twenty-two miles upstream.

1926 Maj. Ulysses S. Grant III, grandson of the eighteenth president of the United States, succeeded Sherrill and presided

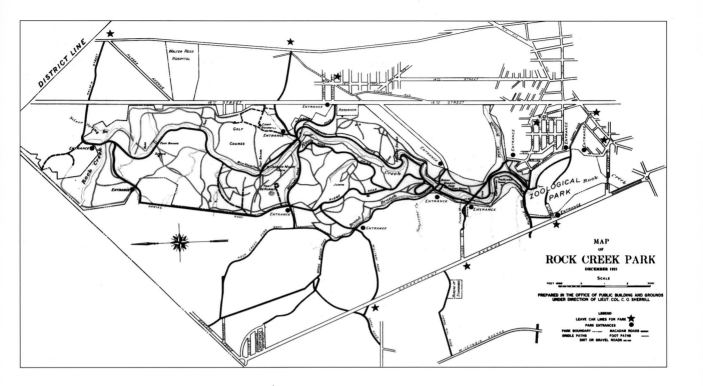

over the park until shortly before military administration of the District's buildings and parks ended in 1933.

Tennis courts on Park Road east of the Beach Drive intersection were built.

1933 Established in 1916, the National Park Service assumed leadership of Rock Creek Park. An executive order by President Franklin D. Roosevelt abolished the Office of Public Buildings and Public Parks of the National Capital, and the Rock Creek and Potomac Parkway Commission, and assigned their mandates to the Department of the Interior's Office of National Parks, Buildings, and Reservations—the new but short-lived name for the National Park Service. Rock Creek Park became part of National Capital Parks, headed by C. Marshall Finnan until 1939. Interim heads succeeded him until 1941, when Irving C. Root, former chief engineer with the Maryland

Sherrill's map of Rock Creek Park, 1921. Courtesy of the National Archives Still Picture Division, 66-G-23R-56.

National Capital Park and Planning Commission, became superintendent, a post he held until 1950. A line of career Park Service managers followed.

1935   The Park Police Lodge was built.

1936   President Franklin D. Roosevelt dedicated the Jusserand memorial bench south of Peirce Mill. The memorial honors French Ambassador Jules Jean Jusserand (1855–1932), who spent much of his career in the United States and was appreciated for his dedication to improving French and American relations. A story is told about his skinny-dipping caper in Rock Creek with President Theodore Roosevelt and a few others. After a strenuous hike, the men stripped down and were about to jump into the water when the President noticed that Jusserand still wore his climbing gloves. When he asked why, the ambassdor replied, "In case we meet ladies."

1937   The former Brightwood Reservoir along Sixteenth Street was filled, and the land was made available for sports fields and recreation.

1950   Carter Barron Amphitheatre was built.

1957   The Horse Center on Glover Road was built.

1958   The Park Police Stables and Maintenance Yard were built.

Military Road was widened to a four-lane freeway.

1960   The Nature Center and Planetarium on Glover Road opened.

1960s–'70s   Paved bicycle routes were introduced.

1977   Following an administrative reorganization, Rock Creek Park became an organizational unit of the National Park System and is responsible for ninety-nine parks and reservations, including Meridian Hill, Glover and Archbold Park, Battery Kemble Park, Dumbarton Oaks, Civil War fortifications, and the Rock Creek and Potomac Parkway.

1987   The William H. G. Fitzgerald Tennis Stadium was built at the Brightwood location (Sixteenth and Kennedy streets, NW). [23]

Rock Creek Park, undated photograph. Courtesy of the National Archives Still Picture Division, 66-G-23U-54.

Park Flora

Hundreds of plant species grow in Rock Creek Park, the majority indigenous and the rest introduced, many during the era of Joshua Peirce, Washington's leading horticulturist in the nineteenth century. Eighty-five percent of Rock Creek Park is natural forest, much of it second growth, partly resulting from heavy land clearing during the Civil War, when a wide swath of land connected the city's forts; Fort DeRussy stood at the highest point in the park.

Today, the National Park Service aims to protect the park from further non-indigenous plant invasion. The park's flora has been classified according to plant associations, or species that grow in groups. Of the park's top four plant groupings, listed below, the beech—white oak/mayapple group predominates. The map on page 55 shows the location of all of the park's plant associations. [24]

Beech—White Oak/Mayapple Forest

Canopy	white oak, beech, and tulip poplar
Subcanopy	white oak, beech, tulip poplar, other oaks, hickories, black gum, flowering dogwood, and sparse American holly
Shrub layer	maple-leaved viburnum
Herbaceous	mayapple, jack-in-the-pulpit, poison ivy, Christmas fern, cucumber root, squawroot, sweet cicely, false Solomon's seal, wild yam, tick-trefoil, and partridgeberry
Exotics (nonnatives)	garlic mustard, Japanese honeysuckle, and Asiatic bittersweet

Tulip Poplar Forest

Canopy	tulip poplar
Subcanopy	tulip poplar and/or box elder
Shrub layer	spice bush and blackberry
Herbaceous	absent
Exotics (nonnatives)	multiflora rose, porcelain berry, and lesser celandine

Span, 2002, by Elżbieta Sikorska, mixed media, 45 x 60 in. Courtesy of the artist.

Chesnut Oak—Black Oak/Huckleberry Forest (on dry ridges)

Canopy	chestnut oak and black gum; sparse red and black oak and red maple
Subcanopy	sassafras, serviceberry, greenbrier, and grape vine
Shrub layer	heaths including azalea, blueberry, mountain laurel *(kalmia),* and huckleberry
Herbaceous	sparse or absent
Exotics (nonnatives)	few species

Sycamore—Green Ash Forest (on flood plains)

Canopy	sycamore and box elder; red maple and tulip poplar often co-dominant
Subcanopy	green and white ash and hickory frequent associates; bladder-nut and river birch occasional associates
Shrub layer	spicebush and occasional black haw
Herbaceous	jewelweed, mild water-pepper, jack-in-the-pulpit, enchanter's nightshade, skunk cabbage, and poison ivy
Exotics (nonnatives)	garlic mustard, lesser celandine, English ivy, stilt grass, multiflora rose, and Japanese honeysuckle

Left to right: Diospyros virginiana. Deciduous Trees—Winter Outline. National Arboretum, March 21, 1975, unknown photographer. Courtesy of the Horticulture Services Division, Smithsonian Institution. Botanical illustration of "Common Tulip Tree," from A. B. Strong, *The American Flora,* vol. III (New York: Hull & Spencer, 1855), 56. Courtesy of Smithsonian Institution Libraries, Horticulture Branch.

Opposite: Map showing the park's plant associations. Courtesy of the National Park Service, Rock Creek Park.

Common Tulip-tree

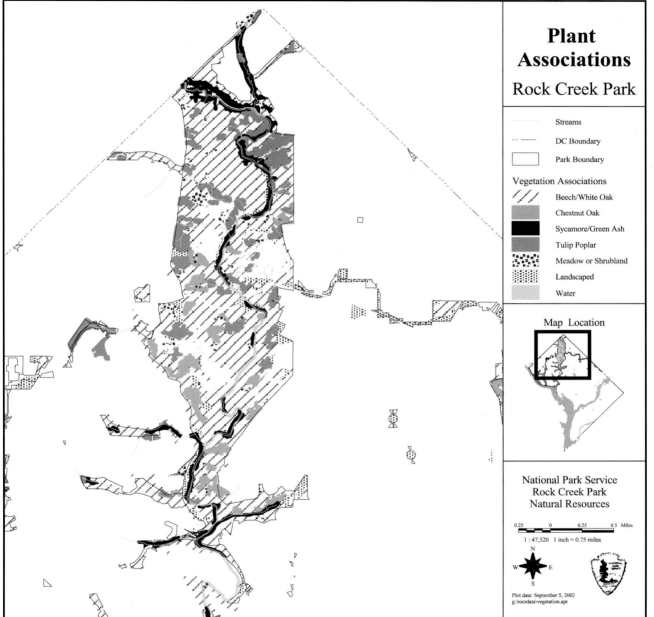

Plant Associations

Rock Creek Park

	Streams
	DC Boundary
	Park Boundary

Vegetation Associations

	Beech/White Oak
	Chestnut Oak
	Sycamore/Green Ash
	Tulip Poplar
	Meadow or Shrubland
	Landscaped
	Water

Map Location

National Park Service
Rock Creek Park
Natural Resources

0.25   0   0.25   0.5   Miles

1 : 47,520   1 inch = 0.75 miles

N
W   E
S

Plot date: September 5, 2002
g:\rocrdata\vegetation.apr

Bridges

Many bridges cross Rock Creek, and some of Washington's most famous bridges—Connecticut Avenue's Taft and Q Street's Dumbarton, or "Buffalo," bridges—are not in the park proper but built along Rock Creek and Potomac Parkway. The Sixteenth Street Bridge, nicknamed Tiger Bridge for its four sphinxlike tigers sculpted by Alexander Phimister Proctor in 1910, crosses Piney Branch at the park's eastern arm near its southern boundary. The bridge is in the same neoclassical tradition as the Taft and Dumbarton bridges and was the first parabolic concrete arch bridge built in the United States.

Numerous park bridges serve cars, pedestrians, or horses. Many original bridges have been removed, renovated, or replaced. Pre-1933 wooden bridges, such as the once popular Old Rustic Footbridge, on line with Blagden Avenue, were temporary structures that often washed away. Peirce Mill's bridge is the oldest, dating to 1872. Since then, it has undergone several renovations, including its conversion to steel.

Boulder Bridge (1902), on Beach Drive north of the Broad Branch Road intersection, is Rock Creek Park's principal icon. Its oversized, rounded stones have a distinctly man-made look in an otherwise perfectly natural setting, although the stones do come from the creek. The melan-arch bridge, whose design is credited to William J. Douglas, crosses Rock Creek at the site of the dam for the former Argyle (Bladgen) Mill, once located about four hundred yards downstream. According to park lore, the contract for the bridge's construction called for "man-size" stones, a technical term for stones light enough to be handled by a worker without machinery. However, the contractor of Boulder Bridge took the term man-size literally, and because it took several hours by carriage to reach the work site from downtown government offices, construction was well under way before Col. Lansing H. Beach, in charge of the park, "drove out to observe the progress. The work was so well advanced, and too, the large boulders made such an attractive voussoir to the arch, that it was thought advisable not to change to the smaller 'man-size' stones that had been intended, although even then it would have been less expensive to have used the smaller stones to finish the bridge." Some of these voussoir stones weighed more than one thousand pounds. [25]

Boulder Bridge, from the Rock Creek Park Report of 1918. Courtesy of the National Park Service, Frederick Law Olmsted National Historic Site. 2837-54

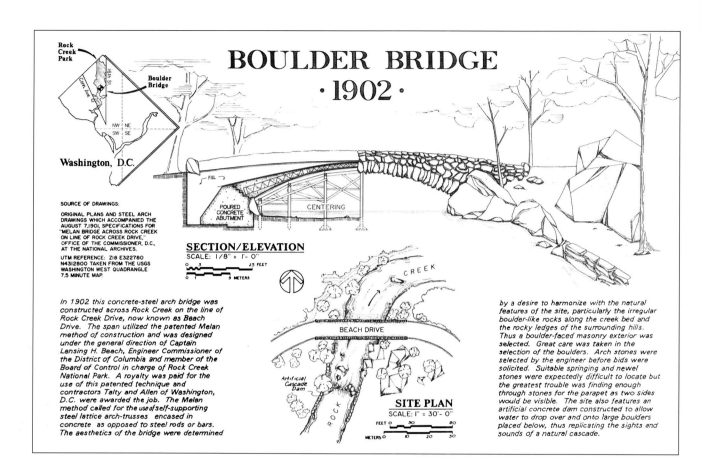

BOULDER BRIDGE
·1902·

Rock Creek Park

Boulder Bridge

Washington, D.C.

SOURCE OF DRAWINGS:

ORIGINAL PLANS AND STEEL ARCH
DRAWINGS WHICH ACCOMPANIED THE
AUGUST 7,1901, SPECIFICATIONS FOR
"MELAN BRIDGE ACROSS ROCK CREEK
ON LINE OF ROCK CREEK DRIVE,"
OFFICE OF THE COMMISSIONER, D.C.,
AT THE NATIONAL ARCHIVES.

UTM REFERENCE: ZI8 E322780
N4312800 TAKEN FROM THE USGS
WASHINGTON WEST QUADRANGLE
7.5 MINUTE MAP.

FILL

POURED
CONCRETE
ABUTMENT

CENTERING

SECTION/ELEVATION
SCALE: 1/8" = 1'- 0"

0   5   25 FEET

0   1   5 METERS

CREEK

BEACH DRIVE

Artificial
Cascade
Dam

ROCK

SITE PLAN
SCALE: 1" = 30'- 0"

FEET 0   30   90

METERS 0   10   20   30

In 1902 this concrete-steel arch bridge was
constructed across Rock Creek on the line of
Rock Creek Drive, now known as Beach
Drive. The span utilized the patented Melan
method of construction and was designed
under the general direction of Captain
Lansing H. Beach, Engineer Commissioner of
the District of Columbia and member of the
Board of Control in charge of Rock Creek
National Park. A royalty was paid for the
use of this patented technique and
contractors Talty and Allen of Washington,
D.C. were awarded the job. The Melan
method called for the use of self-supporting
steel lattice arch-trusses encased in
concrete as opposed to steel rods or bars.
The aesthetics of the bridge were determined
by a desire to harmonize with the natural
features of the site, particularly the irregular
boulder-like rocks along the creek bed and
the rocky ledges of the surrounding hills.
Thus a boulder-faced masonry exterior was
selected. Great care was taken in the
selection of the boulders. Arch stones were
selected by the engineer before bids were
solicited. Suitable springing and newel
stones were expectedly difficult to locate but
the greatest trouble was finding enough
through stones for the parapet as two sides
would be visible. The site also features an
artificial concrete dam constructed to allow
water to drop over and onto large boulders
placed below, thus replicating the sights and
sounds of a natural cascade.

Ross Drive's open-spandrel reinforced bridge, completed in 1907 and also designed by Douglas, diverged from the melan-arch style of the park's earlier bridges. Although the bridge was widened in 1968, its historic design integrity remains intact.

Designed by the influential Washington architect Glenn Brown in 1902, the popular Pebble Dash Bridge (with pebble finish) crossed Broad Branch at its juncture with Rock Creek. The bridge was replaced in the 1960s.

Among the park's unique features are its old fords, Klingle and Milk House fords the best known and used well into the twentieth century. Milk House Ford—also called Rock Creek Ford at one time—is still operable but is gated and preserved as a park relic. In 1929, Military Road's bridge replaced Milk House Ford as the principal crossing at that location. The crossing for Klingle Ford Road (today's Klingle Road) lies in line with present-day Porter Street. Other fords served equestrian trails north of Sherrill Drive. [26]

Carriages crossing a park
ford, early 20th century.
Courtesy of the National
Archives Still Picture
Division, 66-G-234-92.

Rock Creek Park, Rapids Footbridge, 1988, by Jet Lowe. Courtesy of the Library of Congress, Prints and Photographs Collections.

Page 62: From Robert L. Dickinson, "Washington Walk Book," 1918. Unpublished notebook with sketches. Courtesy of the Library of Congress, Prints and Photographs Collection. Used by permission of Dr. Robert L. Dickinson's grandchildren.

Page 63: Stone Bridge, Rock Creek Park, by Lucien Whiting Powell (1846–1930), watercolor on paper. Courtesy of the Collection of Richard B. Fuller. Landscape artist Lucien W. Powell studied in Philadelphia with Thomas Moran and at the Pennsylvania Academy of Fine Arts. He later studied at the London School of Art and was influenced by the landscape style of J.M.W. Turner (1775–1851). He was a native of the Washington area and his works are in the National Gallery of Art, the Corcoran Gallery of Art, and other collections.

Spring in Rock Creek
Park

Visitor Information

Washington residents and tourists are encouraged to visit Rock Creek Park's web site for current programs, news, and events at: www.nps.gov/rocr. Information also can be obtained by e-mailing ROCR_superintendent@nps.gov or by calling the headquarters at 202.895.6000. The visitor information line is: 202.895-6239.

Rock Creek Park comprises 1,754 acres, most of which are undisturbed woods along both sides of the meandering creek. It is open seven days a week during daylight hours and offers the following recreational facilities and visitor centers:

The Nature Center and Planetarium
- Wednesday through Sunday, 9 A.M. to 5 P.M.
- Closed Mondays, Tuesdays, and federal holidays
- 5200 Glover Road, NW, in the park
- 202.895.6070

The park's first Nature Center occupied the Klingle Mansion from 1956 to 1959. Today's Nature Center, located on the site of a former caretaker's residence, opened in 1960 and offers year-round educational programs, nature programs and expeditions, planetarium shows entitled Night Sky and Exploring the Universe, and a discovery room for children. Some popular interpretive programs include Animal Olympics, Turtle Talk, Creature Feature, and Fort DeRussy hikes; well-attended educational programs are Sensory Stroll, Water Quality, Be a Junior Naturalist, and Habitat Hunt. Visit the web site for the monthly schedule of programs.

Picnic Grounds
Rock Creek Park's thirty picnic sites are available for group gatherings. Twenty sites are first-come, first-served for groups of less than fifteen people. Ten picnic areas, a few with shelters, can be reserved for up to seventy-five people through the Department of Parks and Recreation at 3149 16th Street, NW, 202.673.7646. Two picnic permits per area are issued per day, one for the A.M. and one for the P.M., and cost ten dollars. The park's map is available online and at the Nature Center and Peirce Mill, and it indicates picnic locations: sites marked with blue circles must be reserved. More information may be obtained by calling 202.673.7646.

Hikes
The park is laced with paths affording sylvan views and peaceful respite from city

Photograph, undated, from the *Star* Collection, copyright *Washington Post,* permission of the D.C. Public Library.

life; the main paths derived from old farm roads. National Park Service maps are available at the park's visitor sites. Volunteers from the Potomac Appalachian Trail Club (PATC) help the park maintain the trails, and its detailed map is available at local outfitters shops and book and map stores. It can also be obtained from the club's web site store at www.patc.net. For more information on the club's maps and resources visit their web site or call PATC headquarters at 703.242.0693.

Biking, Jogging, Roller Blading, and Walking

The park offers a paved bicycle path, which connects to paths in Maryland and Virginia; however, on weekdays, from Broad Branch Road to the Maryland line, bikers share Beach Drive with automobile traffic. On weekends and holidays, sections of Beach Drive are closed to vehicle traffic and rapidly fill with bikers, roller bladers, joggers, and strollers, all sharing the open space between tall trees and the exhilarating freedom of a natural landscape. Bingham and Sherill Drives are also closed to motorists on weekends and holidays. Barry Mackintosh's book *Rock Creek Park: An Administrative History* (see bibliography) offers a detailed history of the bike paths development from the early 1960s.

Rock Creek Park Horse Center

- Tuesday through Friday, 2 to 8 P.M.
- Saturday and Sunday, 10 A.M. to 5 P.M.
- Closed Mondays and federal holidays
- Next door to the Nature Center at 5200 Glover Road, NW, in the park
- 202.362.0117

Bridle paths and riding were part of Rock Creek Park from the beginning, and today thirteen miles of trails crisscross the park. The Horse Center is the District's only full-service equestrian stable and offers trail rides, riding lessons, pony rides, summer camps, and boarding facilities. Barry Mackintosh's book on Rock Creek Park (see bibliography) describes in detail the park's equestrian history.

Peirce Mill

- Wednesday through Sunday, 12 P.M. to 4 P.M.
- Closed Mondays, Tuesdays, and federal holidays
- Beach Drive and Tilden streets, NW
- 202.426.6908

Peirce Mill (1829) is Rock Creek Park's—and the city's—only surviving grist mill and is an excellent example of the region's vernacular stone architecture. Although the mill ceased operation in 1897, over the next century it continued to be used, first as a tea house and then as park offices. From 1935 to 1936 the National Park Service restored it, but by 1958 it had to be closed again. Following a second restoration in 1967, Peirce Mill became operable once more, and tourists could witness a nineteenth-century flour mill in action. The mill is currently in need of repairs, and a citizens group, Friends of Peirce Mill, has been raising funds to restore the machinery. In the meantime, educational programs and group tours are available.

Peirce Barn (the former Art Barn and Art Gallery)

- Saturday and Sunday, 12 P.M. to 4 P.M., closed Monday thru Friday
- Next door to Peirce Mill

Peirce Barn is one of several barns built by Isaac Peirce (1756–1841), the original owner of Peirce Mill and the land surrounding it. From 1971 to 2002, this charming stone building was known as the Art Barn and offered art exhibitions. Now under National Park Service operation, the barn hosts exhibitions on the mills of Rock Creek Valley and the history of the Peirce estate.

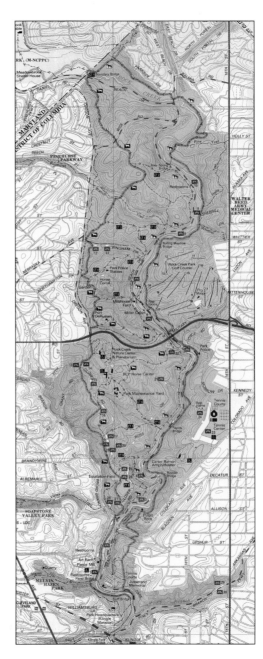

Map adapted from a hiking map (PATC Map N) and used with permission of the Potomac Appalachian Trail Club (PATC). www.patc.net *67*

Carter Barron Amphitheatre

- 4850 Colorado Avenue, NW (16th Street and Colorado)
- 202.426.0486

In June, the Shakespeare Theatre offers free performances of Shakespeare's plays under the stars and surrounded by Rock Creek Park's whispering trees. The theater is considered by some environmentalists as one of the greatest park intrusions, and yet Washington audiences respond rapturously to the midsummer night's magic of open-air theater. In 1949, Congress passed legislation allowing the National Capital Sesquicentennial Commission to erect structures for the 150th anniversary celebration of Washington as the nation's capital. Secretary of the Interior Oscar L. Chapman approved the Rock Creek Park site for a large amphitheater and extensive parking lot. The theater opened in 1950 under the administration of the sesquicentennial commission, whose executive vice chairman was Carter T. Barron. He died soon after the theater opened, and so it was thought befitting to name it after him.

Tennis

For many Washingtonians, the sprawling tennis center at 16th and Kennedy streets, NW, is the most glaring park intrusion; however, this tract of land had already been cleared in 1900 for the Brightwood Reservoir that in 1937 was filled to devel-

op for recreational use. Today, ten hard- and twenty soft-surfaced tennis courts are available for play April through mid-November and can be reserved for a fee through Guest Services, Inc.: 202.722.5949. The hard-surface courts are available the rest of the year on a first-come, first-served basis, free of charge. On Park Road, across Beach Drive from Peirce Mill, three soft-surface courts are available May through September, and reservations can be made in person at the courts.

Ball Fields and Playground

At 16th and Kennedy streets, NW, adjacent to the tennis center, several fields suitable for soccer, football, and field hockey can be reserved through the District's Department of Parks and Recreation. This "pleasure ground" also has a playground and sheltered picnic area (no. 24), the latter of which must be reserved (see Picnic Grounds, page 65). For information on ball field permits, call 202.673.7449.

Rock Creek Golf Course

- Open sunup to sundown daily, except Christmas
- Sixteenth and Rittenhouse streets, NW
- 202.882.7332

The 108-acre site for the course was chosen in 1921 because it was preexisting farmland and would require minimal clearing. Two nine-hole courses were completed in 1923 and 1926, respectively, with changes made to the tees, greens, and traps over the century. The golf course was one of the first intrusions into the park's natural integrity. President Woodrow Wilson, a frequent visitor to Rock Creek Park, opposed the golf course plan in a letter to Rock Creek Park's officer in charge:

Is it possible that it is true that a golf course is to be laid out in Rock Creek Park? I am loathe to believe that such an unforgivable piece of vandalism is even in contemplation, and therefore beg leave to enter my earnest and emphatic protest.

That park is the most beautiful thing in the United States, and to mar its natural beauty for the sake of a sport would be to do an irretrievable thing which subsequent criticism and regret would never repair.[27]

Construction of Carter Barron Amphitheatre, 1949. National Park Service, permission of Washingtoniana Division, D.C. Public Library.

Lower End of Rock Creek Park, 1891, attributed to M. B. Waite. Courtesy of the Historical Society, Washington, D.C.

Notes

1. Material for this section on Washington's early history came from William Bushong's *Historic Resource Guide, Rock Creek Park* (Washington, D.C.: National Park Service, United States Department of the Interior, 1990), chaps. 2 and 3. The Civil War period population statistics came from John Reps, *Monumental Washington: The Planning and Development of the Capital Center* (Princeton: Princeton University Press, 1967), 53.

2. The history of Michler's survey can be found in Barry Mackintosh, *Rock Creek Park: An Administrative History* (Washington, D.C.: National Park Service, United States Department of the Interior, 1985), 3.

3. Ibid., 10.

4. Cornelius W. Heine, "The Contributions of Charles Carroll Glover and Other Citizens to the Development of the National Capital," *Records of the Columbia Historical Society* (1953–56): 229–48.

5. Mackintosh, *Rock Creek Park,* 8.

6. Ibid., appendix.

7. Perry Wheelock, National Park Service Cultural Resource Specialist, conversation with author, March 9, 2002.

8. Adrienne Coleman, Superintendent of Rock Creek Park, conversation with author, March 15, 2002.

9. Frederick Law Olmsted Jr., "Landscape in Connection with Public Buildings in Washington," in *Papers Relating to the Improvement of the City of Washington* (Washington, D.C.: Government Printing Office, 1901), in Papers of Glenn Brown, American Institute of Architects.

10. The history in this chapter is an amalgam of information found in several sources including John W. Reps' three books, *Washington on View: The Nation's Capital Since 1790* (Chapel Hill: University of North Carolina Press, 1991); *Monumental Washington*; and *The Making of Urban America: A History of City Planning in the United States* (Princeton: Princeton University Press, 1965); U.S. Congress, Senate, Committee on the District of Columbia, *Improvement of the Park System of the District of Columbia,* ed. Charles Moore (Washington, D.C.: Government Printing Office, 1902) (nicknamed the McMillan Plan); Lt. Col. Ulysses S. Grant III, "The L'Enfant Plan and Its Evolution," *Records of the Columbia Historical Society* (1933–34): 1–23; Frederick Gutheim and Wilcomb E. Washburn, *The Federal City: Plans and Realities* (Washington, D.C.: Smithsonian Institution Press and the National Capital Planning Commission, 1976); Bushong, *Historic Resource Guide;* and Mackintosh, *Rock Creek Park.*

11. Newton B. Drury, "Frederick Law Olmsted: His Monuments Are All about You," *National Parks Magazine* 32, no. 133 (April–June 1958): 58.

12. Charles Moore, "Makers of Washington," unpublished manuscript, quoted in Susan Klaus, "Intelligent and Comprehensive Planning of a Common Sense Kind: Frederick Law Olmsted, Junior and the Emergence of Comprehensive Planning in America, 1900–1920" (master's thesis George Washington University, 1988), 75. Other facts in this biographical sketch also came from a reading of Klaus's thesis and from William H. Tishler, *American Landscape Architecture: Designers and Places* (Washington, D.C.: Preservation Press, 1989), 60–65.

13. Drury, "Frederick Law Olmsted," 59.

14. Ibid., 60.

15. Edward Clark Whiting and William Lyman Phillips, "Frederick Law Olmsted—1870–1957: An Appreciation of the Man and His Achievements," *Landscape Architecture* 48, no. 3 (April 1958): 155.

16. Ibid., 145.

17. The first quotation is from Olmsted Sr. to Olmsted Jr., 24 December 1894, and the second is from an undated letter of the same period, both in the Frederick Law Olmsted Papers, quoted in Klaus, "Intelligent and Comprehensive Planning," 47–48.

18. Drury, "Frederick Law Olmsted," 62.

19. Information for this biographical sketch came from Witold Rybczynski, *A Clearing in the Distance: Frederick Law Olmsted and America in the 19th Century* (New York: Simon and Schuster, 1999), and Tishler, *American Landscape Architecture,* 38–43.

20. Frederick Law Olmsted to John Charles Olmsted, December 1, 1877, John C. Olmsted Collection, Frances Loeb Library, Graduate School of Design, Harvard University, quoted in Rybczynski, *A Clearing in the Distance,* 334. Another source used for this biographical sketch was Tishler, *American Landscape Architecture,* 48–51.

21. Rybczynski, *A Clearing in the Distance,* 334.

22. All of the excerpts are taken from Olmsted Brothers' "Rock Creek Park: A Report," December 1918, Frederick Law Olmsted Papers, Manuscript Division, Library of Congress.

23. The sources used to compile this chronology were Barry Mackintosh's *Rock Creek Park: An Administrative History* and William Bushong's *Historic Resource Guide.*

24. This list of Rock Creek Park's plant associations was developed from data in the Nature Conservancy's "Vegetation Classification of Rock Creek Park," unpublished paper (Arlington, Va.: The Nature Conservancy, March 1998).

25. Zack Spratt, "Rock Creek's Bridges," *Records of the Columbia Historical Society* (1953–56): 101–34.

26. Spratt, "Rock Creek's Bridges"; Bushong, *Historic Resource Guide,* 108–12; 173–80; Donald Beekman Myer, *Bridges and the City of Washington* (Washington, D.C.: Commission of Fine Arts, 1974).

27. Mackintosh, *Rock Creek Park,* 34.

72

Selected Bibliography

For researchers, the National Park Service, Rock Creek Park, has a photographic archive that was not available to me but is supposed to resurface for public use at an unspecified date in the future.

Books

Beveridge, Charles, comp. *The Master List of Design Projects of the Olmsted Firm, 1857–1950*. Boston: National Association for Olmsted Parks in conjunction with the Massachusetts Association for Olmsted Parks, 1987.

Bushong, William. *Historic Resource Guide, Rock Creek Park*. Washington, D.C.: National Park Service, United States Department of the Interior, 1990.

Gutheim, Frederick, and Wilcomb E. Washburn. *The Federal City: Plans and Realities*. Washington, D.C.: Smithsonian Institution Press and the National Capital Planning Commission, 1976.

Klaus, Susan L. "Intelligent and Comprehensive Planning of a Common Sense Kind: Frederick Law Olmsted, Junior and the Emergence of Comprehensive Planning in America, 1900–1920." Master's thesis, George Washington University, 1988.

Kohler, Sue A. *The Commission of Fine Arts: A Brief History, 1910–1995*. Washington, D.C.: U.S. Government Printing Office, 1996.

Kohler, Sue A., ed. *The Senate Park Commission Plan for Washington, D.C., 1901–1902* (working title). Washington, D.C.: Commission of Fine Arts, 2002 (forthcoming).

Mackintosh, Barry. *Rock Creek Park: An Administrative History*. Washington, D.C.:

National Park Service, United States Department of the Interior, 1985.

Myer, Donald Beekman. *Bridges and the City of Washington*. Washington, D.C.: Commission of Fine Arts, 1974.

Nature Conservancy. "Vegetation Classification of Rock Creek Park." Unpublished paper. Arlington, Va.: Nature Conservancy, March 1998.

Olmsted, Frederick Law, Jr., and Theodora Kimball, eds., *Frederick Law Olmsted, Landscape Architect, Early Years and Experiences: The First Volume of Forty Years of Landscape*. Vol. 1. New York: G. P. Putnam's Sons, 1922.

Olmsted, Frederick Law, Jr., and Theodora Kimball, eds. *Frederick Law Olmsted Senior: Forty Years of Landscape Architecture: Being the Professional Papers of Frederick Law Olmsted, Senior*. Vol 2. New York: G. P. Putnam's Sons, 1928.

Olmsted Brothers. "Rock Creek Park: A Report." December 1918. Frederick Law Olmsted Papers, Manuscript Division, Library of Congress.

Peterson, Jon A. *City Planning in the United States, 1840–1917: The Birth of a Comprehensive Vision*. Baltimore: Johns Hopkins University Press, forthcoming, 2003.

Reps, John W. *The Making of Urban America: A History of City Planning in the United States*. Princeton: Princeton University Press, 1965.

———. *Monumental Washington: The Planning and Development of the Capital Center*. Princeton: Princeton University Press, 1967.

———. *Washington on View: The Nation's Capital Since 1790.* Chapel Hill: University of North Carolina Press, 1991.

Roper, Laura Wood. *FLO: A Biography of Frederick Law Olmsted.* Baltimore: Johns Hopkins University Press, 1973.

Rybczynski, Witold. *A Clearing in the Distance: Frederick Law Olmsted and America in the 19th Century.* New York: Simon and Schuster, 1999.

Schuyler, David. *The New Urban Landscape: The Redefinition of City Form in Nineteenth-Century America.* Baltimore: Johns Hopkins University Press, 1986.

Sies, Mary Corbin, and Christopher Silver. *Planning the Twentieth-Century American City.* Baltimore: Johns Hopkins University Press, 1996.

Stenzel, Franz, M.D. *James Madison Alden: Yankee Artist of the Pacific Coast, 1854–1860.* Fort Worth: Amon Carter Museum, 1975.

Tishler, William H., ed. *American Landscape Architecture: Designers and Places.* Washington, D.C.: Preservation Press, 1989.

U.S. Congress, Senate, Committee on the District of Columbia. *Improvement of the Park System of the District of Columbia.* Ed. Charles Moore. Washington, D.C.: Government Printing Office, 1902.

Articles and Reports

Bugbee, Mary F. "The Early Planning of Sites for Federal and Local Use in Washington, D.C." *Records of the Columbia Historical Society* (1951–52): 19–31.

Clark, Allen C. "Charles Carroll Glover." *Records of the Columbia Historical Society* (1939): 141–52.

Drury, Newton B. "Frederick Law Olmsted: His Monuments Are All About You." *National Parks Magazine* 32, no. 133 (April–June 1958): 58–62.

Fleming, Peggy, and Raclare Kanal. "Annotated Checklist of Vascular Plants of Rock Creek Park, National Park Service, Washington, D.C." *Castanea* 60, no. 4 (December 1995).

Grant, Lt. Col. Ulysses S. III. "The L'Enfant Plan and Its Evolution." *Records of the Columbia Historical Society* (1933–34): 1–23.

Heine, Cornelius W. "The Contributions of Charles Carroll Glover and Other Citizens to the Development of the National Capital." *Records of the Columbia Historical Society* (1953–56): 229–48.

The Nature Conservancy. "Vegetation Classification of Rock Creek Park." Unpublished paper. Arlington, Va.: Nature Conservancy, March 1998.

Olmsted, Frederick Law, Jr. "Landscape in Connection with Public Buildings in Washington." In *Papers Relating to the Improvement of the City of Washington.* Washington, D.C.: Government Printing Office, 1901. Papers of Glenn Brown, American Institute of Architects.

Olmsted, Frederick Law, Jr., and John Nolen. "The Normal Requirements of American Towns and Cities in Respect to Public Open Spaces." *Charities and the Commons* 16, no. 14 (July 1906): 411–26.

Peterson, Jon. "The Hidden Origins of the McMillan Plan for Washington, D.C., 1900–1902." In *Historical Perspectives on Urban Design.* Ed. Antoinette J. Lee. Occasional Paper No. 1. Center for Washington Area Studies, George Washington University, 1983.

Scott, Mel. "The Heyday of the City Beautiful." Chap. 2 in *American City Planning Since 1890: A History Commemorating the Fiftieth*

Anniversary of the American Institute of Planners. Berkeley: University of California Press, 1969.

Shoemaker, Louis P. "Historic Rock Creek." *Records of the Columbia Historical Society* (1912): 38–52.

Spratt, Zack. "Rock Creek's Bridges." *Records of the Columbia Historical Society* (1953–56): 101–34.

Whiting, Edward Clark, and William Lyman Phillips. "Frederick Law Olmsted—1870–1957: An Appreciation of the Man and His Achievements." *Landscape Architecture* 48, no. 3 (April 1958): 145–57.

Zihlman, Frederick N. "History of the National Capital and Work of the National Capital Park and Planning Commission." Speech delivered to the House of Representatives, February 28, 1927. Washington, D.C.: Government Printing Office, 1927.

Rock Creek © 2002
Nicolynn Green. Courtesy
of the photographer.

Acknowledgments

I have Katy and Herman Woerner to thank for arranging my first visit to the Olmsted National Historic Site on the same day that the Rock Creek Park Report of 1918 had been pulled from off-site storage to display for a special event. This coincidence may have had divine intervention. Katy and Herman have offered me encouragement, respect, wisdom, and love over many years, and this book, like so much of my work, is interwoven with their lives.

Michele Clark, archivist at the Olmsted site, provided continuous, patient research assistance, which helped make this book become reality. Her colleague Michael Dosch answered many of my early inquiries. Perry Wheelock, the National Park Service's cultural resource specialist for Rock Creek Park, served as my guide throughout the project, sharing her expertise, resources, and time. Laura Illige, Rock Creek Park's chief ranger, acted as my liaison to park resources and from the beginning underwrote the project. I am also grateful to Superintendent Adrienne Coleman for taking time to talk to me about the park's future. Other Rock Creek Park and Olmsted specialists provided expertise for this book, including

Barry Mackintosh, Sue Salmons, Alan Banks, Dwight Madison, and Dan Wining.

At the Historical Society of Washington, D.C., Gail Redmann helped me find photographs and old records related to the park's history. Many other archivists in Washington's many rich repositories searched databases and led me to appropriate collections for the materials used in this book, and I thank them all. Paula Healy at the Smithsonian's Horticulture Division, Susan Raposa and Sue Kohler at the Commission of Fine Arts, Carol Johnson at the Library of Congress, and Peggy Appleman at the Martin Luther King Jr. Memorial Library, in particular, contributed time and expertise to my work. I cannot imagine this project without the enthusiastic response and help from members of the Potomac Appalachian Trail Club, including Dave Peirce, who allowed his trail map to be adapted for these pages, and past president Phil Barringer. In addition, many local artists and art collectors shared their paintings, new and historic, of Rock Creek Park; Barbara Nuss, president of the Washington Society of Landscape Painters, Sarah Turner at the American Institute of Architects, Richard Fuller, Mary Kokoski,

Andrei Kushnir, Nicolynn Green, and Harold Dorwin, in particular, generously provided artwork for this book.

The creativity, artistic spirit, charm, and rare sensibility of designer Yael Kats infuse the pages of this book; she was a trusted and enthusiastic collaborator from the very beginning.

I was able to complete this book thanks to the leave of absence generously granted me by the Freer Gallery of Art and Arthur M. Sackler Gallery at the Smithsonian Institution. Among the many colleagues and friends who listened to my progress reports on the book, I am particularly grateful to Brenda Tabor, Nancy Hacskaylo, Bruce Tapper, Kathleen Burke, Karen Sagstetter, Jeffrey Thompson, and Howard Kaplan. Howard's insightful reading of the first draft steered me toward a stronger product. Jennifer Alt's expert copyediting improved the manuscript, and Suzanne Crawford generously helped proofread the layouts. I am grateful to editors at the Johns Hopkins University Press who saw merit in my project and set the wheels of production in motion.

Gratitude goes to my parents, sons, siblings, and greater family for their commitment, creativity, passion, and laughter; my life and work have drawn from this bountiful source.

Rock Creek, © 2002 Nicolynn Green. Courtesy of the photographer.

Overleaf: Photograph from the Rock Creek Park Report of 1918. Courtesy of the National Park Service, Frederick Law Olmsted National Historic Site. 2837-52

Rock Creek Park in Spring,
2002, by Andrei Kushnir,
oil on canvas, 14 x 18 in.
    Courtesy of the artist.

A Note on the Type

Yael Kats designed *Rock Creek Park* in Bembo, a typeface based on Francesco Griffo's design for another book with a beautiful natural setting, Pietro Bembo's Sicilian sojourn *De Aetna,* published by Aldus Manutius in 1495. In 1929 Stanley Morison resurrected the typeface for the Monotype Corporation, and like Rock Creek Park, Bembo has preserved its beauty, popularity, and appeal.